Praise for *The Joy Exchange*

"Laura reminds us that joy isn't something you stumble upon—it's something you exchange, moment by moment, with the people right in front of you. This book is a love letter to belonging, and it shines a light on the beauty we discover when we stop rushing past and start paying attention. You'll laugh, tear up, and maybe even change the way you live your Tuesdays."

—**Bob Goff,** *3X* New York Times *bestselling author*

"Java Joy is a magnificent charity and well named too, since their charges create literal joy as witnessed at our various fundraising events in London. Taking center stage; all power to them and to the hard-working people enabling this charity to thrive. This book perfectly captures the beautiful outcomes possible when people are invested in rather than ignored."

—**The Brothers Trust,** *the charity of Tom Holland and his family*

"There are books that inspire, and there are books that transform. *The Joy Exchange* does both. Laura has written something that will resonate whether you're a parent, a leader, or simply someone longing to live with more compassion. Joy, she reminds us, is the thread that can weave us all together."

—**Brittany Sjogren,** *Founder/Visionary, Loverly Grey*

"With *The Joy Exchange*, Laura invites us to imagine what our lives could look like—and what our world could look like—if we chose to love those around us in simple, everyday ways, with welcoming smiles, open arms, and generous hearts. For more than 20 years, she has found and shared untold joy, hope, and meaning in a life devoted to seeing and celebrating the inherent dignity, worth, and beauty of our neighbors with disabilities. I believe her story has the power to transform lives and communities, if we have the boldness to seize more opportunities to love, uplift, and edify others with our words, actions, and attitudes."

—**Dan T. Cathy,** *Chairman, Chick-fil-A, Inc., Founder and Chief Visionary, Trilith*

"As a coach, I've learned that the best lessons don't just come from the scoreboard; they come from people who teach us about resilience, perspective, and joy. Laura Hope Whitaker's *The Joy Exchange* captures those lessons beautifully. This book is a playbook for living with purpose and recognizing the strengths in everyone around us."
—**Kirby Smart,** *Head Football Coach, University of Georgia*

"Laura Hope Whitaker has written a book that overflows with the type of joy that everyone needs to feel in their life. In *The Joy Exchange*, she shares stories that remind us that the greatest teachers are often the most unexpected people, a lesson we have learned firsthand through our time with ESP. This book is not just about perspective—it's about transformation, community, and the kind of hope we all need."
—**David and Lindsey Pollack,** *Former ESPN College Football Analyst and NFL Linebacker; Co-founder of the Pollack Family Foundation*

"I've been blessed to know Laura Whitaker and Extra Special People since my days at the University of Georgia back in 2010. What started as a simple introduction has grown into one of the most meaningful relationships of my life. Laura's heart, vision, and leadership have shaped ESP into a place where kids of all abilities are seen, celebrated, and given opportunities to shine.

This book is Laura's story, but it's also the story of the thousands of kids and families who have been touched by ESP. Having my own small part in that journey is an honor I'll always cherish.

Laura pours herself into everything she does, and this book is no different—it's inspiring, authentic, and full of hope. If you want to be reminded of the power of love, community, and faith in action, you'll find it in these pages."
—**Aaron Murray,** *Former University of Georgia Quarterback, SEC Network Analyst, esp National Board Member*

"Laura has a gift for finding joy in the smallest places and magnifying it for maximum impact, and our small town is proof of that. In *The Joy Exchange*, her words invite us to see life with fresh perspective and remind us that the simplest acts of love and kindness can multiply far beyond what we imagine. In Watkinsville, we make no small plans, and that is largely because we have benefited from the lessons Laura shares in this book—how to live with more connection, gratitude, and purpose."
—**Brian Brodrick,** *Mayor, City of Watkinsville*

"Laura Whitaker is one of the finest, most respected nonprofit leaders in the state of Georgia. I'm so blessed to call Laura a friend. This book, unique in its storytelling as well as perspective, captures the essence and impact of ESP so beautifully. It's a much-needed ray of sunshine for our world today. I predict you will receive a major dose of joy that could change your approach to life by reading it."

—**Glen Jackson,** *Co-founder of Jackson Spalding,*
Author of Preeminence

"*The Joy Exchange* is a breath of fresh air, an invitation to unguarded hearts and abundant joy. Laura Hope Whitaker gently nudges us forward into curiosity, growth, and new friendships. She awakens the best parts of who we are: the childlike part, the open-to-new-friendship part, the seeing-the-world-with-wonder part. Get ready for a dose of delight as you swap old ways of thinking for new ways of being. It's an exchange well worth making."

—**Elizabeth Laing Thompson,** *Author of*
When God Says, "Wait" *and many other books*
for women and teens

TREY AKRIDGE

the joy exchange

*Jill,
Enjoy! Rich &
Laura Hope-Whitman*

Laura Hope Whitaker

Finding Life's
Greatest Lessons
in Those You
Least Expect

WILEY

Copyright © 2026 by Extra Special People Inc. All rights reserved.

Published by John Wiley & Sons, Inc., Hoboken, New Jersey.

No part of this publication may be reproduced, stored in a retrieval system, or transmitted in any form or by any means, electronic, mechanical, photocopying, recording, scanning, or otherwise, except as permitted under Section 107 or 108 of the 1976 United States Copyright Act, without either the prior written permission of the Publisher, or authorization through payment of the appropriate per-copy fee to the Copyright Clearance Center, Inc., 222 Rosewood Drive, Danvers, MA 01923, (978) 750-8400, fax (978) 750-4470, or on the web at www.copyright.com. Requests to the Publisher for permission should be addressed to the Permissions Department, John Wiley & Sons, Inc., 111 River Street, Hoboken, NJ 07030, (201) 748-6011, fax (201) 748-6008, or online at http://www.wiley.com/go/permission.

The manufacturer's authorized representative according to the EU General Product Safety Regulation is Wiley-VCH GmbH, Boschstr. 12, 69469 Weinheim, Germany, e-mail: Product_Safety@wiley.com.

Trademarks: Wiley and the Wiley logo are trademarks or registered trademarks of John Wiley & Sons, Inc. and/or its affiliates in the United States and other countries and may not be used without written permission. All other trademarks are the property of their respective owners. John Wiley & Sons, Inc. is not associated with any product or vendor mentioned in this book.

Limit of Liability/Disclaimer of Warranty: While the publisher and author have used their best efforts in preparing this book, they make no representations or warranties with respect to the accuracy or completeness of the contents of this book and specifically disclaim any implied warranties of merchantability or fitness for a particular purpose. No warranty may be created or extended by sales representatives or written sales materials. The advice and strategies contained herein may not be suitable for your situation. You should consult with a professional where appropriate. Further, readers should be aware that websites listed in this work may have changed or disappeared between when this work was written and when it is read. Neither the publisher nor authors shall be liable for any loss of profit or any other commercial damages, including but not limited to special, incidental, consequential, or other damages.

For general information on our other products and services or for technical support, please contact our Customer Care Department within the United States at (800) 762-2974, outside the United States at (317) 572-3993 or fax (317) 572-4002.

Wiley also publishes its books in a variety of electronic formats. Some content that appears in print may not be available in electronic formats. For more information about Wiley products, visit our web site at www.wiley.com.

Library of Congress Cataloging-in-Publication Data is Available:

ISBN: 9781394375943 (Cloth)
ISBN: 9781394375950 (ePub)
ISBN: 9781394375967 (ePDF)

Cover Design: Wiley
Cover Image: Suzanne Goossens
Author Photo: Courtesy of Laura Hope Whitaker and Suzanne Goossens

To. . .

my greatest teachers—those in these pages and those for whom there weren't enough—I see your abilities, and the world needs them.

my team, past, present, and future—your sleeves rolled up turned dreams into reality.

my friends and family—thank you for leaning in with unwavering generosity.

my greatest joys—#LoveLikeJoseph, Owen, Finley, and Tate.

God—for the gift of this place and people, the spirit to sustain, and a purpose for life. Waiting in anticipation for the ultimate Welcome Wagon.

Contents

Foreword   xv

Section One: Awkward to Aha—1

0   The Dandelions—3

1   The Burst
What Happens When We Exchange Awkward for Awe?—11

2   The Extra Seat
What Happens When We Exchange Avoidance for Action?—19

3   The Chance
What Happens When We Exchange Self-Promotion for Service?—27

4   Sticky Note Soup
What Happens When We Exchange Inadequacy for Initiative?—33

5   The Blind Date
What Happens When We Exchange Hubris for Humility?—41

6   The Hulk
What Happens When We Exchange Empathy for Compassion?—49

7 The Flip Turn
What Happens When We Exchange Comfort for Connection?—57

Section Two: From Invisible to Invaluable—63

8 The Hope Cup
What Happens When We Exchange Hard for Hope?—65

9 The Stage
What Happens When We Exchange Power for Perspective?—77

10 The Brags
What Happens When We Exchange Inability for Ability?—87

11 The Jump
What Happens When We Exchange Cowardice for Courage?—97

12 The Pink Hard Hat
What Happens When We Exchange Invisible for Invaluable?—107

Section Three: From Them to Us—119

13 The Welcome
What Happens When We Exchange Hesitation for Hospitality?—121

14 The Blend
What Happens When We Exchange a Problem for a Purpose?—133

15 The Hug
What Happens When We Exchange a Culture for Connection?—143

16 The Spread
What Happens When We Exchange Moments for Movements?—155

17 The Miracle
What Happens When We Exchange Silos for Shared Spaces?—167

18 The Top Bunk
What Happens When We Exchange Walls for Ramps?—179

19 Enjoy
What Happens When We Exchange Small Things for Big Love?—189

Epilogue: Welcome to Holland—*197*

The Invitation—*199*

Notes—*201*

Acknowledgments—*205*

About the Author—*207*

Index—*209*

Foreword

You will have the most
Heartwarming Gift
To Read This book
of Our All Abilitys
From Extra Special
People.

You will be so Blessed
and Thankful To have
a Special book

All The Happiness

Suzanne

☺ happy Faces

FRieNDsihp

be KiND Faith
Love Sriprts
the Book
ECT.

Love Amber Leigh Young ♡

I think people
should read this
book.
with love
Megan

When you read the book you will be inspired. it shows usus a family- hopefully engaged and wanting to be a part of something special.

LiLy

The Resion wHy people to Read this Book is the Book is magicke

xoxo
Nicky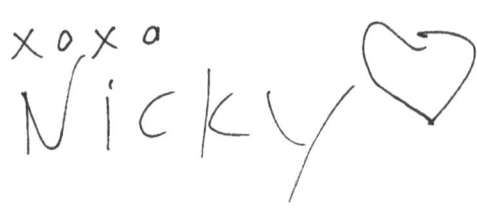

To have the ~~to~~ book be inspiring for you and your family to support.

Elizabeth Cicerchia

SECTION ONE

Awkward to Aha

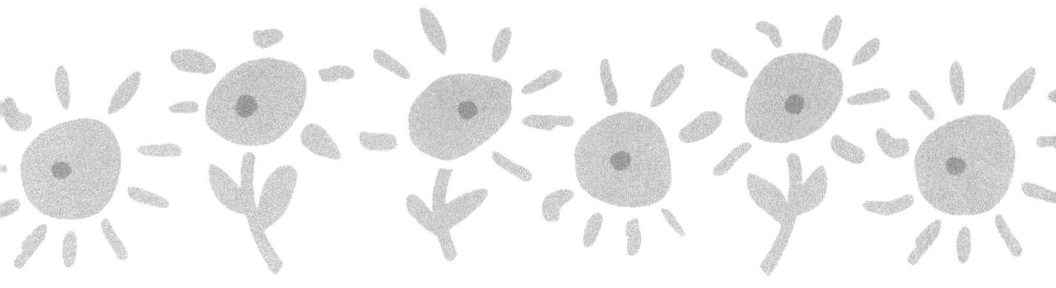

CHAPTER 0

The Dandelions

I used to pick dandelions when I was little.
Did you?
The little yellow flowers that pop up in the yard.
The ones that you pick to weave into a crown or gather to bring to your mom in a bouquet.
The ones that expand into rounded seed form, ready to be blown away on a wish.
As a child, I looked at those dandelions as I did any other flower: a beautiful, colorful creation.
But somewhere along the way, I learned that dandelions are weeds.
Maybe you did too.
They're the poster child for RoundUp weed killer on every home improvement store shelf in the country. It's unfortunate publicity for a plant that once carried magic in its seeds. And not just for children.
For centuries, dandelions were used for medicinal purposes. In many countries, dandelions are grown to be consumed in salads. Bridgestone is raising dandelion farms even now, and because of their strength, they put them in tires. Sometimes we don't learn more as we grow older. Sometimes we lose sight of life's greatest

lessons—like the ones about the dandelions. Are dandelions mere weeds? Or are they a treasure in disguise? The answer depends on who you ask.

When we are children, we treat the uniqueness of items like dandelions with welcomeness and wonder, like gifts to be unpacked or treasures to be discovered. We do the same with the uniqueness of people. We play interchangeably with others on the playground regardless of differences in skin color, accent, or ability.

Then, somewhere along the way, we learn that these differences between us are unsettling, even threatening. . .something to avoid. We become awkward at best, adversarial at worst. Now, as adults, our differences separate us on Sundays and fill our news channels with skepticism and hatred for those not like us.

How do we get back to the magic we once knew?

Look Back

If you were like me, you stepped off the longer bus—the "cheesewagon" as it's called today—as a kindergartner with your backpack and lunchbox. As you walked into school, you looked back, and the shorter bus pulled up to unload the students in wheelchairs, with metal crutches attached to their arms or students holding onto the rail unloading with a slower pace. You entered your classroom on your own volition, while the other students were led to the trailer in the back of the school.

What did that tell you? What did that communicate inadvertently to your young five-year-old brain?

Maybe you grew up in a Christian household. You were taught to love all people, and when you showed up to Sunday school every week, the only people in your class looked like you. Without a single word, what might that have taught you?

Maybe your family had all you needed when you were growing up. And as you left the grocery store in a car full of food, you passed someone asking for a meal. Your parents kept driving. What message did that send?

We all had at least one of those experiences while growing up—probably more than one if we're being honest, because such experiences are common. Over time, the experiences wired our brains to think about and respond to different people with uncertainty, detachment, and even apathy. I think when we survey the landscape of society today, most of us can acknowledge that our handling of our differences has gone too far. We recognize that we're raising the next generation in a world filled with the fog of social angst. And yet, I believe most of us have a deep desire to rewrite this narrative, if not for the whole world, at least for our own families and the world of our daily existence. The time is right. The time is now.

We live in a culture craving belonging and connection yet are starving for examples to follow. In the pages to come, I'd like to invite you into my story and introduce you to a few of my friends who can provide the most beautiful examples. The only way to truly rewrite our stories is to rewire our brains. The only way to rewire how our brains perceive and react to our differences is to experience different people in a new light—in this case, people who offer more joy, love, and belonging than you might have ever imagined they could. The joy exchange has changed countless lives already. I'm betting it will change yours too.

Fast-Forward

We were standing in downtown London at the iconic Claridges Hotel with ballgowns and tuxedos surrounding us. Champagne was presented on silver trays as important bodies shuffled around each other. As we passed through the crowd to find our table, our nerves grew knowing we would finally meet him in person. On screen, in interviews, on Instagram, and during our video calls, he was so kind, welcoming, authentic. But would he be the same in real life? In this setting with the who's who of the philanthropy world?

We paused as he approached and recognized our faces from afar. His body relaxed, and his grin widened. His wavy hair bounced as he strode toward us.

"Nicky, Liz, Laura. . .Mom," he recited one by one. "The Java Joy team is here!"

We introduced ourselves awkwardly, as if he did not just say our names. It felt necessary when meeting someone like him—Spiderman, Tom Holland—who must meet people all the time. Hugs were exchanged around the circle.

"Make yourself at home," he encouraged. "Tonight is going to be fun!"

The gala was full of individuals who had given substantial philanthropic investment to Tom's foundation, The Brother's Trust. As we found our seats and took time to snap a few photos, the evening began. The Holland family hosted a beautiful music trivia night. Tom and his comedic dad, Don, emceed. Tom's brother, Sam, made an appearance from the kitchen as one of the distinguished chefs. Tom's other brother, Paddy, showcased his incredible art that was part of the silent auction. Nikki, Tom's mom, worked the room with her camera, using her keen eye to capture every moment. Yet, as I watched her professional dance, I caught her slipping into occasional proud grins as she watched her favorite men each do his thing.

The food was delicious, and the show interactive and entertaining. Yet, even as the drinks flowed, the room felt a bit stiff. I wondered if it was the celebrity effect. Or maybe the crowd of 200 people felt too small. Or was it that the attendees were from all over the world and we were acclimating to a variety of cultures and accents?

Then, just as I was wondering, it happened.

During a musical pop quiz, the pianist began playing a familiar tune. A song recognized by almost any ear, graced with regal history but turned legendary by Leonardo DiCaprio and Kate Winslet in the movie *Titanic*. As the notes rang out to Celine Deon's "My Heart Will Go On," I could hear the poignant lyrics and Celine's haunting voice in my head. I knew the same was probably true for every person in the room.

The melody climbed.

My emotions followed.

I was lost in a movie scene.

Then, as the pianist approached the chorus, I broke from a mindless gaze to see Nicky, my friend turned colleague, a large African American man with autism, staring at me with eyes of hope and anticipation. Every fiber of his body language was asking me if he should follow his instincts. I shrugged my shoulders in a *I don't know why not?* Kind of way and whispered, "Go for it."

He leapt from the table and skated across the room, mouthing the words of his favorite song of all time: Celine Deon's "My Heart Will Go On." His corn rows swung from side to side, their shells bedazzled and clinking together for added drama. His thick, 6-foot-3-inch body squeezed through the tightly placed chairs, bumping every other attendee in his path. His 16-dollar Crown Jewel souvenir necklace swung back and forth. By the time he reached the stage, the entire room was watching. And Tom's open arms were ready for his company.

The pianist grinned and continued with more vigor now as Nicky took the stage and positioned himself on the front edge, facing the audience, arms wide and reaching out to the chilly Atlantic Ocean, with Tom directly behind him in renowned Titanic stance. Unashamed and in full character, the duo belted out the remainder of the song to our delight and amazement.

When the pianist hit the final note, chairs shot back, and the room jumped to a standing, cheering ovation. Tom's face illuminated with a huge smile as they embraced one another, and then Nicky made his way back to the table, exchanging high-fives, hugs, and fist bumps the entire the way.

Like that, the air in the room had changed. It was lighter, warmer, freer. Bodies relaxed. Smiles came easy and spread from table to table. The energy was palpable. . .like warm sunlight on our skin.

Joy was everywhere.

As the night continued, I watched the single experience multiply in warm glances, lively conversations, hearty laughs, and generous hugs that hadn't existed before Nicky and Tom's impromptu karaoke performance. When the event concluded, there was a longer line to meet Nicky than even his famous, theatrical counterpart. And Tom would not want it any other way. A man with autism had changed the course of the night for everyone.

I found myself thinking, *Who am I to be experiencing such beauty?* It felt like just yesterday that I was an inexperienced college student taking the helm of a small nonprofit organization. Now here I was, watching hundreds of hearts filled with joy from an experience that is available to most of us every single day. We just have to know where to find it, because it usually occurs outside our typical view.

It was not until I found Extra Special People, Inc. (ESP), that I fully understood this. ESP is a nonprofit organization, scaling throughout the southeast United States and soon the country, that exists to create transformative experiences for people with disabilities and their families, changing communities for the better. At age 18, I walked in fully aware of my deficits and uncertainty. Would I say the right thing? Handle the awkwardness the right way? Would I offend someone?

I did not have enough experience.

Then I engaged with people who looked, acted, and responded differently than I did: people with disabilities, some mild and others so profound they could communicate only through movements. In their embrace, the feelings I had when I walked in melted away.

By leaning into the awkwardness, I found a life-changing aha.

I found a joy that I didn't know was available to me.

Now I want to make it available to you.

Take the Invitation

This book is for you, the leader who is longing for more joy for yourself and your organization. For you, the college student who is isolated but whose heart longs for community. For you, the mom who is raising typically developing children but longs for her children to not only receive but learn to give. For you, the professional living a life transactionally who is looking for a more meaningful exchange.

Researcher Matthew Kuan Johnson, a philosopher and cognitive scientist at Oxford, noted that despite substantial and relevant work that has come from positive psychology in recent decades, "surprisingly little work has been done by this field on joy."[1]

According to Johnson, people find experiences of joy difficult to articulate. In his work, he hypothesizes that the very nature of joy pushes the boundaries of our ability to communicate about lived experience via a spoken language.

My two decades of work at ESP tell me he is describing something we can all attest to. I've daily observed people leaving our offices or events with the afterglow of their experience. While difficult to articulate in words, the closest description we have for it is joy.

What is joy?

I describe it as light.

Unable to touch. Unable to grasp.

But when it enters our beings, it radiates from our skin to our souls.

It fuels a sense of purpose.

It illuminates life's meaning.

"With joy," says Brené Brown, "colors seem brighter, physical moments feel freer and easier, and smiling happens involuntarily."

I have learned from the most unexpected people that joy is neither a feeling nor a circumstance.

It is also not happiness.

Joy is an exchange.

My friends at ESP have shown me this. Their experience of life is not tainted by culture's expectations, filters on Instagram, or society's definitions of success. Much like a child with a dandelion, what is seen is good, wonderful, and beautiful to see, not what someone or something told them to see. They have taught me, and many others, that to connect genuinely with someone who doesn't see, hear, or process the world like you is to exchange apprehension, misconception, and judgment for profound joy. And this exchange is available to each of us.

"If you want to get warm," wrote C.S. Lewis, "you must stand next to the fire. If you want to get wet, you must get into the water. If you want joy, power, peace. . .you must get close to, or even into, the thing that has them."

Our souls long for joy, especially in these times we're living in. This is a book about how to step closer to, or even into, the places where it exists in abundance. But like the dandelion, such places are not always where you'd expect.

CHAPTER 1

The Burst

What Happens When We Exchange Awkward for Awe?

> *"Learn the language of your soul's voice, intuition."*
> —Unknown

Slosh the Coke

I have a terrible memory. It's one of my finest qualities: only the moments that matter stay.

One of them unfolded on a family trip to New York City when I was eight.

We were hurrying toward Central Park.

From where?

I have no idea.

To do what?

Still nothing.

I just remember the wind knifing between skyscrapers, the crowds of people scurrying everywhere, and how my little legs struggled to keep up as I gripped my dad's hand beside my older sister.

That's when I saw him.

The Joy Exchange

A man sat on a red blanket, back braced against a stone building. His wheelchair sagged beside him like a collapsed tent. One hand rested on the blanket's fleece; the other rattled a dissolving paper McDonald's cup.

His clothes were torn, and his body was pretzeled. But his eyes were impossibly blue and bright, and they met mine as we walked by. I pulled back on my dad's hand, trying to gain his attention.

"Do we have any money?" I whispered.

My dad smiled the way parents do when they're counting seconds. "We're running late," he said, "but on the way back we'll buy him some dinner."

I waved and smiled as we passed the man, hoping to convey some hope that we'd be back soon.

I don't remember what we did in Central Park. I only remember the smell of hot dogs. Beyond that, my senses were caught up in the man with the blue eyes. Who was he? Where was his family? Would he talk to me when we returned? What would I say?

When we left Central Park, I reminded my dad about the meal. We headed to McDonald's and picked up a burger, fries, and an icy Coke. As we stepped back onto the Manhattan sidewalk, I began to walk with purpose, a burst inside of me that felt warm. The Coke was sloshing from side to side as my dad and sister hurried right behind me. The walk wasn't a long one, but it seemed to take longer than I thought it would. Finally, we turned the corner to the street where he was sitting.

I looked at the spot where I thought he'd be sitting. I looked around and up and down the street. No wheelchair.

No blanket.

No cup.

Surely, this was the right place. I looked at my dad; his face told me it was. Except, the man was no longer there. My knees buckled onto the oil-stained sidewalk. Tourists flowed around me while tears fell down my cheeks.

We missed him. We missed our chance.

The moment branded a lesson deep inside my young heart: when you have a burst to connect with another person, don't hesitate. If you do, the opportunity is often gone.

Remember the Gift

As children, we embraced the burst without coaching. We saw a need, felt it in our guts, and acted before spreadsheets or safety lectures intervened. A four-year-old will hand over her last piece of Halloween candy without estimating blood-sugar levels or college savings.

But growing older rearranges the brain's hierarchy. Our left hemisphere (the accountant) begins driving, and our right hemisphere (the poet) slides into the passenger seat as life experience teaches us to avoid hot stoves, oncoming cars, and, unfortunately, messy people. Caution hardens into cynicism, and the sacred gift of intuition is muffled by the servant of analysis.

Albert Einstein called out this switch a half-century ago: "The intuitive mind is a sacred gift and the rational mind a faithful servant," he wrote. "We have created a society that honors the servant and has forgotten the gift."

Whenever we cross the street to dodge discomfort, scroll past a cry for help, or excuse ourselves with data on panhandlers' statistics, we place another hand over that intuitive voice until it barely whispers. The good news is that neuroscience has upended the old dogma that adult brains are fixed.

Functional MRI shows neural circuits rewiring every day. When you obey one burst, you spark a brand-new pathway of possibilities; keep obeying bursts and you braid a highway of habit. This isn't age-specific. You can dial intuition up to full volume at any age. Or you can ignore it and shut down those synapses of greater possibility.

The truth is that healthy living isn't intuition versus reason; it's intuition-led, reason-guided. Picture that your phone pings and your friend's biopsy came back malignant. Intuition says, *Go now*. Halfway there doubts rise: *What if she's sleeping? What if she doesn't want visitors?* Reason quickly offers structure: *Call from the driveway; leave soup on the porch*. But intuition keeps the car pointed to her street. That's a sort of wise burst that's worth following.

A few years after missing the man in Manhattan, I had another opportunity to follow such a burst, and it changed the trajectory of my life.

Look for Another Chance

I had known Allie since middle school. Her hair was rarely combed, she had a distinct smell, and she was prematurely developed. I had two classes with her that year—PE and art—but she was in a special class for everything else. I always tried to smile at her when I could, but I was not sure how to interact with her. My heart yearned to be kind, but the awkwardness of not knowing what to do got in the way.

Until one day in the cafeteria during our sophomore year of high school.

Allie approached two popular boys wearing their football jerseys and sitting at the popular kids' table by the windows. I was taking a seat at an adjacent table and noticed what appeared to be an unusual interaction about to occur.

I positioned myself out of the boys' line of site and partially shielded by a large trash can but close enough to hear what was transpiring.

Wearing her best velcro shoes and a striped shirt tucked into high-waisted jeans, she began to flirt with the boys. My stomach began to churn. I knew these boys, and I hoped they'd be kind. Then I overheard the word "prom" come from her mouth.

Oh my gosh, no. She is asking them to prom!

"Sure, I'll go with you," one boy said as tried to hide a smirk.

"Me too!" said the other, and then they looked at each other with sarcastic grins.

Allie missed the cues. She grinned back and went in for a hug. In her mind, she had scored not only one but two of the most popular boys in school as her prom dates. Just as her outstretched arms reached them, the boys turned their backs and burst into laughter.

She stood there confused. Then I watched as her look of jubilation suddenly turned to heartbreak.

That's when I felt it.

The burst.

No analytical reasoning stopped me. Despite the boys being my friends and the fact that the entire lunchroom was watching, my intuitive reasoning compelled me to act. Perhaps because I had missed the man with the red blanket and wheelchair nearly half a life before.

I stood up from my seat, grabbed the trash can in front of me, and smashed it against the boys' table. Food flew everywhere, including all over them. I forced back the lump in my throat and choked out, "You should be the ones embarrassed. I hope you remember this!"

I grabbed Allie's hand and walked her straight out of the cafeteria and to the principal's office. We both sat there and cried.

I did not eat my lunch that day. I didn't need to. My soul had been filled with a different kind of nourishment that was even better than food—perhaps more necessary too.

The truth is that Allie and her velcro shoes would have probably recovered without me. I am sure this was not the first time she was hurt by the social complexities that both life and high school offer. But I would have missed the gifts of a new friend and a new aliveness in my soul. I would have also missed an opportunity to meet a calling.

That same year, I began taking a course to complete a teacher-in-training program. They assigned me to a preschool special education classroom with a teacher ready to go on maternity leave, which allowed me to lead the class in her absence. If not for Allie and the burst, I would not have entered that room with a newfound perspective on people of all abilities. Listening to the burst opened me up to a community I knew nothing about. This was the real aha gift I received from leaning into an awkward situation.

Awkwardness is not the enemy; it is a radar. Sometimes it warns, *Danger—back away*. More often it invites, *Connection ahead—lean in*. Parents script this code for their children. Kids' bursts are loud: "Mom, can we give him my sandwich?" If we hush them with "Keep walking," they learn to muzzle compassion. But if we explore with "Let's talk to him together," they learn courage that outlives us.

The same is true for leaders. Intuition catches needs before words form. Think of a suddenly silent employee or a teammate's tear-glossed eyes. When leaders look away from these needs, teams copy. When leaders lean into them, cultures begin to change.

Author James Clear notes, "The seed of every habit is a single, tiny decision."[1] Each time we obey a burst we plant a neural seed; seeds repeated become forests. Keep granola bars in the car and ask a name at the stoplight. Sit beside the co-worker who least resembles your mirror. Smile at the parent juggling a wheelchair and groceries. Little decisions, forest of joy.

Your role shapes the practice. If you're a student, invite the overlooked classmate into your project group; community is your native soil. If you're a parent, let your kids choose a charity, pack snack bags, FaceTime a lonely grandparent; their bursts can reignite yours. If you're a leader, pause the agenda when intuition spots discouragement simmering; the spreadsheet will wait, but morale may not.

Rational thinking should protect you, not imprison you. Avoid actual danger, yes, but don't confuse discomfort with danger. Often, mentally assigning labels like homeless, disabled, or opposite party to others flattens our curiosity into conclusion, which shrinks possibility's radius.

My friends with disabilities taught me a rhythm that keeps our intuitive burst alive: Notice → Pause → Approach → Exchange. Notice the person others overlook. Pause long enough for compassion to outrun convenience. Approach with a question; put names before needs. Exchange whatever you both have: a story, a sandwich, a laugh, a fist bump. When you practice this daily, common places like checkout lines and waiting rooms can become sanctuaries of joy.

THE BURST

Bursts are like sparks. Habits are like kindling. New friendships that are formed are like bonfires that continually warm our heart. Culture so often chants, "It's awkward, I'm out." It's time for us as a society to let a louder anthem rise: "It's awkward; I'll lean in. I'm just one step from aha."

Whether you are 17 or 70, the burst still flickers. Fan it whenever you get the chance. Learn basic sign language. Say hello in the grocery aisle. Invite the neighbor whose accent stretches your ear. Expect awkwardness; it means you're stretching yourself in the most important way. And remember that intuition is the gift; reason is the servant. When the gift leads, the world grows kinder, our minds grow wiser, and our stories grow brighter.

Today, if a voice inside you whispers, *Send the text. . . Offer the ride. . . Ask the name. . .*, answer quickly. One decisive act can reroute a destiny, quite possibly your own.

I missed an opportunity on a Manhattan sidewalk when I was eight. Now I fully comprehend what I missed. I don't want to ever miss an opportunity like that again. I hope you're starting to feel the same. Lean into those intuitive bursts when they come—awkwardness and all—and discover the joy exchange waiting on the other side.

CHAPTER 2

The Extra Seat

What Happens When We Exchange Avoidance for Action?

"Things won are done, joy's soul lies in the doing."
—William Shakespeare

Buy the Glasses

My parents always kept an extra seat at our house when I was growing up.

Best friend, lonely church visitor, kid from down the street—whoever needed dinner was welcome, even in a house that already held six chairs full. Grungy camping weekends, marathon church obligations, and big Southern meals mattered far more to my parents than fancy cars or vacation homes (shout-out to our 1980s Astro van). Dad was a project engineer; Mom worked as a mother-baby nurse at the hospital. Raising me, my older sister Grace, and younger siblings Kathryn and Nathan was enough. And yet, without lecturing, they taught me that family is anyone who finds themselves needed and that tables are meant to expand.

Every parent I know wants inclusive children. No mom rocks a newborn thinking, *I hope she learns to exclude.* Yet what our kids one day project is not what we preach; it is what they experience. Psychiatrist Bruce Perry, writing with Oprah, says, "We elicit from the world what we project into the world; what you project is based on what happened to you as a child."

That truth sobered me as a mother. If dinner tables are always exclusive, children assume that is safety. If tables flex for new faces, children assume that is normal. The baseline forms early and then hums in the background until someone intentionally rewires it.

One rewiring story began over Pinot Noir at my friend Angie's birthday. Between lighthearted conversation, she described a problem her young daughter was having on the school bus. Her second-grader Cora had a new friend—different skin tone, different abilities, same delight in rainbow pens. The friend had Down syndrome. For months Cora came home giddy about her new friend. Then one afternoon the friend punched her face on the school bus. Cora was stunned and hurt, and Angie, understandably, was angry. Mother-bear instinct whispered the standard prescriptions: separate the girls, file a report.

But Angie paused and leaned in instead.

Around the table we replayed the scene and someone asked, "Didn't Cora just get new glasses? Maybe her friend is jealous." That single suggestion flung open a door of possibility. Two days later Angie and Cora delivered a gift-wrapped pair of bright plastic frames to the girl's house. The following morning the new friends rode to school snuggled hip to hip, twin glasses sparkling. No more punches, just giggles. That was exactly what her new friend was trying to communicate.

What did Angie model? When difference creates friction, don't retreat; get curious fast. Buying the glasses rewired three brains: hers, Cora's, and a classmate who now felt seen instead of scolded. What we do today is what our children—and teams and neighbors—will one day display.

Somewhere in your orbit I'm betting there is another "glasses" story waiting to be lived out: a class clown masking anxiety, an abrasive co-worker drowning in grief, an elder whose comments reflect hearing loss and not hostility. Will you lean in or label and bolt? My advice is to buy the glasses.

Say It Again

After the incident with Allie and the boys at the table, you'd think I would have remained stronger. Inside, I had grown strength, but insecurity is a formidable force that can keep us from acting on our best intentions. The longing to be accepted by others is one of the most insatiable desires in life. And no one is immune.

Growing up, I was plagued by middle-sister comparison, and by the time I was a student at the University of Georgia, insecurity had migrated to roommate décor. Standing in Brumby Hall I eyed my Bed Bath & Beyond quilt beside designer monograms and felt Brene Brown's "crush of conformity on one side and competition on the other." I wondered how I would match up in this world compared to others. I would find the answer to all of that, but not with a designer pillow case. I would find myself in the place you least expect.

A friend mentioned something called Extra Special People (or ESP for short), a Saturday club 15 minutes off campus in tiny Watkinsville, Georgia. I imagined psychics when I heard ESP, but curiosity trumped skepticism. One fall morning I rumbled past fields in my battered red Accord, windows down and early-2000s rock on the radio, to arrive at a small brick building. Inside was one cavernous room with vinyl tile flooring and on it a handful of college volunteers assembling craft kits.

I scanned the room looking for someone in charge to give me some direction. That's when I noticed a woman with cropped brown hair, Mickey Mouse tee, and red lipstick. Her presence was somehow both serious and radiant. Intimidation almost turned me around, but I forced my feet in her direction. I reached out my hand, but she offered a hug instead.

"I'm Martha," she said. "And you are?"

"Laura. Here to volunteer."

Martha thanked me for coming and gave me a two-minute tour with zero fuss. Right when she had finished explaining how I could help that day, members began rolling in: freckled boys with Down syndrome, a brown-haired girl in a wheelchair pushed by her sister, a lanky teen whose grin flexed wider than his gait. My heart ping-ponged between the burst to engage and the fear of bungling it. Yet every single face beamed. They wanted to be there.

Like Ruthie.

She wore a perfect bob haircut, matching pink tie-dye outfit, and glasses framing her iridescent eyes. Five minutes in, she marched up to me, seized my hand, and declared, "Hi, I Ruthie!" She then shoved a ball into my palm. Clearly she was ready to play.

Conversation flowed as we played though I understood only half her words. When confusion showed, I leaned in—"Say it again, Ruthie?" She'd then repeat it three times, thrilled someone wanted to understand. This was Ruthie's superpower: quickly minimizing the gap between stranger and friend.

Neuroscientist Allan Schore describes that superpower. Studying infant brain development, he found that joy through shared delight in another's face is the fuel for healthy social wiring.[1] Neurotheologian Jim Wilder extends the finding: each of us carries a joy capacity, he explains, but that capacity can grow at any age through repeated moments of mutual gladness.[2] I didn't know the supporting research at 18, but I clearly felt its evidence. The ESP community operated with colossal joy capacity and zero hesitation to engage it. Members like Ruthie were rewiring me faster than any self-help podcast. They knew how to delight. And I wanted to learn.

My insecurities had quickly evaporated. I had shown up there to help others, but here I was feeling like the one being helped, seen, and loved.

At pickup time, caregivers returned wearing softer shoulders than they'd arrived with. "Always winter but never Christmas," C.S. Lewis wrote of Narnia before Aslan reversed the land's curse.[3] I learned quickly that caregiving a child with complex needs can feel that way.

It requires constant vigilance and involves ongoing costs, milestone envy, and chronic uncertainty about the child's future. It's a long, seemingly unending winter. When their children get to spend a few hours at ESP, it can feel like Christmas has finally come to their winters. As I watched caregivers arrive to retrieve their children, buddies greeted them bragging on what their child accomplished, not what they lacked. Parents heard laughter instead of alarms. For maybe the first time, they felt they had a partner who saw and understood them.

After cleaning glitter off tables, Martha gathered the college crew. She pulled out an extra chair for me, the newcomer who almost didn't come. That simple inclusive act felt like rocket fuel to me; I was part of something that mattered deeply, and I wasn't turning back.

"I'll be back next month," I said to Martha as I sat down. "How can I help?"

Martha grinned. "Terrific! You can run the music."

I had no clue what that entailed, but as I thought about Ruthie's fearless grip and her squinty eyes showing a face of undaunted delight, my answer was absolutely yes. I couldn't wait to experience this again; I wanted more of the joy.

Own the Awkward

Why does awkwardness stop so many of us before we experience the shared joy of a social interaction? Philosopher Alexandra Plakias argues that awkwardness only arises during social situations. Her theory is that awkwardness is therefore not an emotion but a social cue—a shared alert that social scripts are absent or inadequate.[4]

Now think about the era we're living in. At a time when we rely on technology for much of our daily communication, it is not surprising that social interactions are becoming more awkward. We live in an age where phones and algorithms have shrunk our social practice fields, so the slightest unscripted moment between us and another person now blares: MAXIMUM DISCOMFORT. We label ourselves, others, or the moment itself as awkward when in fact we are merely untrained on how to respond to those moments. We don't have the scripts to quell the awkwardness. What happens then? We often exit the moment instead of addressing it. And we miss the chance to experience a new joy.

What's the solution?

The cure for awkwardness between you and another person is not a personality transplant. It's simply noticing its presence and then responding with the right words or action. With my friends on the autism spectrum we literally rehearse greetings, eye contact, and conversational give-and-take. Neurotypical adults could use the same simple drills. Many of us are just out of practice.

We all harbor excuses for hesitation, especially with someone we don't know or understand, and each feels reasonable. Yet behind every stalled burst is another lost aha moment:

- When young professionals postpone coffee with a mentor, their fear of awkward feedback blocks growth and connection.
- When adults skip learning a new hobby, their dread of beginner embarrassment undermines friendships waiting at the studio.
- When parents avoid hard conversations with teens, their side-stepping of the cringe robs intimacy and guidance.
- When leaders mask struggle, their team's empathy and cohesion never spark.
- When neighbors don't knock on the widow's door, their opportunities for reciprocity die in silence.

What ultimately hangs in the balance is joy. Shakespeare pinned it when he wrote, "Joy's soul lies in the doing."[5]

Only action converts an intuitive burst into an impactful bonfire.

Run the Music

Driving back to campus that afternoon, I replayed my first morning at ESP. The entire experience—from Martha's warm hug to Ruthie's confident greeting to the lighter smiles on the faces of caregivers at pickup—pointed to the same conclusion: leaning into social awkwardness with a kind initiative can quickly morph into life-giving connection.

I didn't think God needed me at ESP any more than Martha did. I knew anyone could push a play button on a stereo. Yet today I shudder at what I would have missed had I hit Snooze that day. The sights, sounds, and exchanges I experienced rewired my baseline and gave me greater resolve to lean in to awkwardness, not away from it.

I returned the following month and ran the music. It really didn't matter what my role was; I just wanted to be there. And I kept coming, semester after semester, until ESP ceased being a volunteer gig and became my compass. Somewhere between the monthly dance circles and glittery crafts, I realized my college student insecurity had loosened its grip. Comparison had lost its voice with me. I was finding my healthiest, most confident, most joyful self in precisely the place I once feared: the open seat beside people who move and speak and think differently than me. A table had stretched again, just like it had in my home growing up. And this time the open chair had my name on it.

Ultimately, that is the invitation hidden in socially awkward encounters: slide the chair, buy the glasses, run the music. The burst is waiting for action, and so is the joy that follows.

CHAPTER 3

The Chance

What Happens When We Exchange Self-Promotion for Service?

> *"The merger of self-forgetting, where you lose sight of where you end and something else begins, can take you beyond happiness to joy."*
>
> —David Brooks

Rock the Boombox

I lugged my 1990s boombox into ESP Club, popped in a mix-CD of camp classics, and made a complete fool of myself crooning "Skinnamarinky-dinky-dink." It didn't matter that I was off-key; what mattered was the burst that shot through the room when counselors and campers alike twirled, shrieked, and belly-laughed. Leading music had zero to do with talent and everything to do with a willingness to step straight through the hesitation of awkwardness.

I kept coming back. I was addicted to the highs: crazy dance moves, parents exhaling at pickup, the way even the most stoic volunteer eventually jumped up and down screaming "Potato chips!" if they did not know the words. The burst kept spreading, so one spring afternoon I called home and announced I would not be returning to Atlanta for the summer. I was working at ESP Camp.

That decision dropped me into the most transformative summer of my life—eight scorching Georgia weeks with 8–12-year-olds of every shape, color, and ability: known as the Middle-Younger group. We swam, bowled, staged mud wars, and collapsed under fans with red faces and wider smiles. I was more exhausted and happier than I had ever been, falling in love with the person I was becoming.

Each morning we formed a giant circle for our anthem:

> *Extra Special People, that is who we are,*
> *We are E-S-P, you and me.*
> *With courage and with good friends, together*
> *we can make it.*
> *Extra Special People, that is who we are.*
> *We are ESP you and me.*
> *We help out in our cities. And learn some*
> *useful skills.*
> *We just want to contribute. Try us, you'll*
> *be thrilled.*
> *Where people get together to see what*
> *we create.*
> *To build some understanding and better*
> *to relate.*
> *We are a group that refuses to yield. (HUH!)*
> *Extra Special People, that is who we are.*
> *We are ESP you and me.*

The song bled into silly chants, stunts, and a brag ceremony where campers and counselors applauded one another's triumphs from the day before—someone tried broccoli, someone floated on her back, someone shared a paintbrush without prompting. The world could use a lot more circles like that.

On the Friday of Week 2—payday—Martha handed out our first checks. Mine came last. "There's a letter in there, Laura," she said. "Wait 'til you get home to read it."

Lord have mercy, I thought.
I have already messed up my first job.
I cannot get anything right.

Naturally I ripped it open the second I plopped down in my beat-up red Accord. First came the check ($6 an hour—hello, new swimsuit). Then came Martha's handwriting. I took a big breath in, expecting the worst.

But as I began reading, my hands began to shake for another reason.

"I see something special in you," she wrote. "As of Monday, your unit leader will follow you, and you will be the unit leader. You can do this."

I stared at the words in disbelief. Camp hierarchy was a sacred ladder; badges were earned through years of diapers, mud, and song lyrics. I had been here 10 days. And I was going to lead a unit of counselors and kids? And plan the activities? And lead the songs? On Monday?

My sweaty forehead dropped to the steering wheel.

Should I go back inside and remind her I am an insecure freshman from Atlanta, Georgia, who knows nothing about leadership? Should I remind her that this is my second week of my first-ever ESP Camp? Should I remind her there are probably dozens more who deserve this seat more than me?

As I sat there rehearsing my response, Martha's words echoed in my head. . .

"You can do this."

She was taking a chance on me. She was leaning in. Maybe that chance was all I needed.

Impostor syndrome wasn't a buzzword yet, but that's exactly what pressed on my chest as I drove past Martha's shiny red Porsche. Researchers have since observed that chronic self-doubt spikes when experience lags behind opportunity. The cure is not more navel-gazing—most 18-year-olds don't know themselves because their gifts haven't been activated. And activation happens best in places of service, where stakes are real but grace and growth abound.

Martha's leap of faith shoved me onto that activation track. I skipped the new swimsuit and spent my paycheck on cheap sunglasses and a pack of multicolored pens. Then I spent the weekend sketching schedules for my brand-new unit.

The opportunity I was given was not one I had earned, mastered, or even shown actual skill in. It was an opportunity one woman gave me. The opportunity led to experience, and the experience led me to find myself in a way I'd never even imagined.

We live in a culture where service is often seen as either a badge on a transcript or an end-of-life resolution, when we have already accomplished all we want for ourselves. Service is too often something we promise to fit into the gaps of our lives, and often those gaps rarely come.

But what if the exchange of yourself meant you would find yourself? What if the real exchange for service wasn't a transcript badge or a better epitaph? What if the real exchange for service was the discovery of your destiny?

Step into the Lab

The summer that followed Martha's letter was equal parts romance, foam parties, 100-degree pavement, diapers, seizures, and so much joy it spilled out of our sneakers. I spoke softly in leadership meetings and worked loudly—scrubbing tables, hauling wheelchairs, learning every name. Trust came slowly, especially from "the A-team," a cadre of veteran camp counselors whose names all happened to start with A. They'd grown up at ESP, knew every inside joke, and treated me—newbie, outsider, unit leader—as a curiosity more than anything. To be honest, I didn't deserve anything more. I was even more curious than they were.

My own unit earned me a less glamorous nickname: "Pooper Scooper." Colostomy bags, surprise diarrhea, constipation that always resolved itself right after we zipped swimsuits—if it involved the digestive tract, it happened in Middle-Younger. Leadership, I discovered, often looks like cleaning crap. Proverbs phrases it this way: "Where there are no oxen, the manger is clean, but abundant crops come by the strength of the ox."[1] Translation: you want a harvest? Prepare for a mess.

One blistering afternoon at overnight camp I escorted my buddy Brittany—16, hazel-eyed, beautiful smile, and freshly navigating puberty with autism—toward arts and crafts. She'd seized earlier, was overstimulated, and suddenly melted down on the asphalt. Following protocol, I slid behind her into a "pretzel hold" to keep us both safe while she kicked and sobbed. Georgia sun scorched the backs of my legs; sweat stung my eyes. Finally she began to hum Barney's "I Love You"—her apology song. I released the hold, knelt to help her stand, and *wham*—she drove both heels into my ribs.

The breath whooshed out of me. I dropped to one knee just as the A-team zipped by on a golf cart, laughing about some admin errand. They slowed. "You good?"

"Yeah," I wheezed, refusing to show weakness. Pride, I realized, can break a rib faster than any kick. Misunderstandings layered on misunderstandings: they thought I was arrogant; I thought they despised me. None of us voiced it, so assumptions galloped. If I relived that scene today, I'd wave them down, confess my pain, and ask for help. Vulnerability builds bridges; secrecy cements silos.

Another camper named Bryan expanded that discovery. He was 13, dark-skinned with a camera-flash smile, and typed on a speech device because he'd been labeled nonverbal. His parents prayed he'd one day speak at camp. I secretly vowed he'd say at least one word before August.

He adored trains, ranch dressing, and camp songs. Hoping for street cred with campers, I introduced the ridiculous "Tarzan" chant: bang your chest, holler like a lunatic, repeat. Counselors looked mortified. But Bryan lit up like the Fourth of July, pounding his own chest and giggling. From then on he'd tap my shoulder, grin, and thump his sternum. "Say Tarzan," I bribed shamelessly, "and you get extra ranch."

No dice.

On the final week, I guided him onto the bus, hugged his stiff frame, and turned to leave.

"Bye," he whispered.

I looked back, and my heart swelled.

Bryan was smiling from the backseat, as if he had waited the entire summer to make sure he received every single bribe. And then at the last moment, he gave me what he knew I had been waiting for. A trusted exchange of friendship with one simple word.

I learned from Brittney and Bryan that friendship is about connection. I learned from Brittney to listen for the "I'm sorry," because we all say it in different ways. She taught me that we are all misunderstood. What I thought I needed from Bryan was a word, but what I really needed was affirmation and confidence at a time I felt most insecure. He taught me patience in friendship and that even when words are few, love can be big.

I didn't receive these gifts in a classroom or during a sterile internship or on social media or on a podcast.

I received these gifts from others who seemed nothing like me from the outside looking in but were exactly like me on the inside.

What I thought I needed that summer was a triumph for my résumé. What I really needed was affirmation and courage in the midst of misunderstanding and raging insecurity. Martha, Brittany, and Bryan gifted these to me, wrapped in chance, a song, and a single word.

CHAPTER 4

Sticky Note Soup

What Happens When We Exchange Inadequacy for Initiative?

> *"I think, at a child's birth, if a mother could ask a fairy godmother to endow it with the most useful gift, that gift should be curiosity."*
>
> —Eleanor Roosevelt

Take a Step in the Dark

If you have ever worked a summer camp, you know the bond is soldered with sweat, glitter, and inexplicable inside jokes. Bryan, Brittany, Ruthie—every camper became a thread in the tapestry of that first ESP summer. We were so busy chasing water balloons we barely noticed that our "Maff," Martha, was fading.

Only in the last week did her Mickey Mouse grin look thinner. At the end-of-camp bowling party she draped medals around necks, and I saw her eyes dim behind the applause.

That afternoon, after the campers had all returned home and the cleanup had been completed, Martha lined up 30 college counselors on metal chairs that scraped the gym floor. The guys spooned icing straight from the tub. The girls dabbed their last-day-of-camp tears.

When we were settled, Martha walked over, unfolded a chair, and eased into it. Then she told us the devastating news: she'd been diagnosed with Stage IV pancreatic cancer.

Martha had started Extra Special People in 1986 as a recreational haven for people of all abilities. She saw the need for kids with disabilities to be able to leave school and forge friendships and have fun like their typical peers. As the volunteer director, she started ESP with eight families in a local church, moved to an old jail, and ultimately she and her husband built the 1,200-square-foot gym we were sitting in that day. She taught a whole town to sing, "We are E-S-P, you and me."

Now she looked at us college students and said, simply, "ESP—you and me." She didn't talk about her treatment plan or the plan for the organization while she recovered. She knew what we didn't quite grasp—her time was short. Her condensed line was telling us that the torch was now ours.

That October I mailed Martha a letter: "You were the first to believe in me," I wrote. "I hope to be like you one day."

She died three days later, on October 9, 2004. An interim director kept the doors open the next few months, but grief and bills started piling up. The magic was thinning.

Then my phone buzzed during my fall semester finals. It was the interim director. She cut to the chase.

"Laura, will you run camp this summer?"

I was 19. I didn't know much, but I knew enough to know what the real question was: would I lead ESP?

The burst inside me ignited. I remembered the man with the blue eyes, Allie in the cafeteria, and my buddies at ESP. I would not miss the next right thing. And now I'd had some practice.

Sticky Note Soup

Theodore Roosevelt once said, "In any moment of decision, the best thing you can do is the right thing. . .the worst thing you can do is nothing." Awkward inadequacy usually stops us, whispering someone else is more qualified. But what if it's not about qualification?

"Of course," I answered.

The résumé said I was the wrong caretaker. I was a college sophomore who knew nothing about nonprofits, didn't realize we were $50,000 in the red, and had no clue how to hire staff, fix a failing board, or drive a bus. Yet, I accepted the job anyway. Sometimes opportunity arrives when you are blissfully unaware of all you don't know, and just enough ignorance leaves room for initiation and that endangered trait called curiosity.

Add to the Sticky Stack

When we're 5 years old, we ask 300 questions a day; as adults we whittle that to 25. Why? Because questions expose inadequacy. What if we reclaimed them?

To prepare for my new position, I was given four neon sticky notes. I hoped these would give me the magic ingredients to continued success. What I discovered is that on these four sticky notes were the phone numbers for the police chief, the pool manager, the print shop owner, and the board. We all have to start somewhere.

But how would I plan a camp and raise $50,000 with four sticky notes? There was no donor or camper database. The only base I had was the one I was standing on, and I needed a home run.

When we feel inadequate, we have three choices: to shrink back, to look for validation, or to learn. I could not shrink back; people needed ESP. There was no use in looking for validation; it was obvious I was inadequate for the job. So I had to initiate, I had to learn the trade.

But I needed to find people who could teach me.

I made appointments with each person on a sticky note, one by one, in between college classes and practicums.

The police chief introduced me to the mayor. The pool manager and the print shop owner knew everyone. I tried to make more with what I had. I went hands open to anyone I interacted with, and I said, "I do not know what I am doing. Can you help?" Little did I know that these two lines would comprise a secret weapon to many more years of the organization's growth. When you are 19, people know you do not know.

Why do we sometimes pretend we do when we're older?

People who know things often enjoy helping people who willingly admit they do not know things. But to get support, mentorship, and help, you must be willing to expose what you need.

When you are willing to move past the awkward, connect with people authentically, and make an ask for help, you find another gift of aha on the other side.

At our core, people want to help people, not organizations. Whether it is a story, a person who needs support, or the person standing before them with big blue eyes saying, "I need you." At our core is a desire to meet others' basic needs and lean in with support if we can. But ahas don't happen on an Instagram post or LinkedIn update. Genuine social curiosity and the ability to learn from those around you comes from an authentic in-person connection.

As we have become more sophisticated as an organization, I ache not to lose this. The truth is that after nearly two decades of doing this, I need help now more than ever. Whether we are rebuilding a flailing organization, starting one from the ground up, or managing a multimillion-dollar one, missions are carried out by people willing to initiate by opening their hands and saying, "We need help. Will you help?"

The more I was willing to expose my inadequacy and ask for help, the larger my sticky note stack became. But this eventually led to me drowning in work. At the end of the day, I still needed to finish college. I needed to raise funds for camp, put together a human resources notebook for the staff, and try to manage a B in statistics.

Sometimes, we give up on big dreams because we go at them alone, afraid to speak them into existence, afraid to bring other people in. We know we are inadequate, and so we just sit in that. I knew I had a choice in that challenging moment: I could keep exposing my inadequacy and initiate more help, or I could continue on this isolated effort and see if I could make it.

Find the Mentor

One spring day, fully overwhelmed, I decided to go to my major professor for advice on how to do it all. I knocked on her door, and as I peered inside, she looked at me over her computer with her glasses halfway down her nose. She was surrounded by stacks upon stacks of papers. . .all around her laptop, all over her desk, and piling over onto her meeting table and shelves. Her desk resembled my overwhelmed state.

She looked into my eyes, which were now filling up with tears and instantly knew I needed her. I folded into her chair as she came around to hug me.

I told her that I had more work than I knew what to do with. I needed to somehow make it through my sophomore year of college and run a nonprofit.

"I do not know how to do this. I don't know if I can," I said as the tears flowed down my cheeks.

She removed her glasses and smiled. "It is not a question *if* you can do this, Laura. It is *how* you will do this."

She sat with me for the next two hours, sorting and prioritizing my to-do lists. It was the first time I wanted permission to make it through college to focus on bigger things right before me. But I had felt trapped in a way. Or maybe held back is the right description. I wanted to run with ESP—I had ideas, as naive as they might have been—but I felt torn because I didn't feel right about quitting college to do it.

Then my college advisor and professor said something that gave me wings.

"What good is a perfect GPA if you have sacrificed those you love? You have an opportunity to live out the education you are studying. Go for it."

She could see the forest through the trees in a way my exhaustion and inexperience could not. She then advised me to employ one of my classmates to help me with some of the administrative work.

"I can't afford it," I told her.

"You can't afford not to," she replied. I knew she was right.

I approached one of my closest college friends, Alison. She was in my college cohort and was also a counselor at ESP. She was the kind of friend who knits a hat for you when you have a baby. The kind who brings you soup when you're sick. She knew nothing about QuickBooks or HR practices, but she loved me and she loved ESP. That was enough. Hired.

She and I sat at my kitchen table for hours and switched between college courses and camp counselor contracts. It was another few weeks without much pay for me so I could afford her, but it reduced my stress and gave me a sense of camaraderie. She was the support I needed to keep the momentum going in asking for help. Me, her, and our growing pile of sticky notes.

Hiring Alison gave me time to go throughout the community and talk to anyone who would listen. I talked about the deficit and about our doors closing and how that would affect local families. Eventually the newspapers and radio stations began to listen: "Special needs camp to close due to the founder's death unless the community steps up."

Slowly, I could see that my burst was becoming a community outburst.

I am not adequate, I told myself. *But I will find the people who collectively will be.*

Just Don't Cry

Martha had set up the board of directors as an advisory that met once a year. Our board had four members. By this time, however, one member was in jail for embezzlement, another absent, and another lost a son tragically in an accident. The first board meeting involved the fourth member teaching me what a profit-and-loss statement was. This happened right before our big United Way meeting to pitch for continued funding. I was doing the pitching. I will never forget it.

The United Way executives walked in, suited up with leather folders for their notebooks and pretty briefcases. And there I was, a college student in her church dress working through insecurities of sweat stains and acne.

Totally inadequate.

The biggest piece of advice I was given for the presentation was, "Do not cry." I was also told the United Way needed to see self-sufficiency in the organization. The problem was that I was a college student living on her student loans and her parents' dime. I reeked of un-self-sufficiency.

I was shaking as I shared with these professionals the events that had happened since Martha's passing. I told them about the funds we had raised by going to newspapers, radio stations, and local family foundations. I also told them that the camp would close if our community did not rally together. But I was doing everything I could to avoid this.

As I looked every member in the eye, I then dug deep to reflect confidence and vulnerability. I opened my hands and shared the only thing I knew to share: the stories of the people behind the data points.

My board member told me not to cry.

He did not say anything about them crying.

An hour after our meeting began, we shared hugs in the hallway. Like that, I had 10 more sticky notes with names and phone numbers. The collection was turning into something with real potential.

Make the Soup

There's an old tale about a traveling musician who came to a city looking for money and food. He knocked on doors of home after home, looking for food and asking, "Do you have anything spare for me to eat?" He was rejected time and time again. Everyone needed something to eat in that city. Everyone was hungry.

Then he had an idea—a vision for solving the community's shared problem.

He went to the town's river and picked out the smoothest stone he could find. He then borrowed a large pot, put the stone in it, and filled it with water. He made a fire in the center of town and began boiling the pot. As he interacted with the townspeople, they naturally asked him what he was making. "Stone soup!" he told them boisterously, explaining how amazing this soup would soon be. He would then lean in with a softer tone and say to each person, "If only I had a potato," or, "If only I had a carrot," changing to a new item each time that would make the soup better.

To his surprise, people began to help, offering one item at a time. There were potatoes and carrots, then an onion and spices, and, finally, meat. Each villager contributed what they had to the soup until the pot was filled to the brim with the tastiest, heartiest soup anyone could imagine. And best of all, when it was done cooking, there was enough to feed the entire village.

This, I realized, was my job. And this was how ESP would make it. I was like that soup maker, only my soup was made up of dozens of sticky notes that each symbolized a contribution from the community. A carrot here. A cut of meat there.

Soon, my collection of sticky notes was the wallpaper of my apartment. Maybe those four sticky notes that were left behind were more than an inadequate start. Maybe they were purposefully meant to prod me to build a community that would make up for what I could not accomplish alone.

Independence is excellent when it comes to learning a new skill, studying for a test, or getting the job done that has been delegated to you. But sometimes, we also use independence to solve problems that require more than individual grit and resourcefulness. That autonomy often leads to isolation. And the isolation leads to depression, loss of dreams, and ultimately an unfulfilled community.

Albert Einstein once claimed, "I have no special talent; I am only passionately curious."[1] I stapled that quote above my desk. Then the week after the United Way meeting, I took one of the executives to lunch. She mentioned a utility-bill "round up" fund, and then she offered to help me. We wrote the grant request together and secured our first $20,000. My sticky-note soup was now simmering into something that could nourish Martha's original vision.

And maybe it could nourish even more.

We are Extra Special People, you and me. Not because any of us is wholly adequate, but because together—adequacies and inadequacies, abilities and disabilities—we comprise something extraordinary that no one could produce alone.

And it all begins when we exchange personal inadequacy for relational initiative.

CHAPTER 5

The Blind Date

What Happens When We Exchange Hubris for Humility?

> *"True humility is something totally different; it is the feeling of oneness.*
> *Humility means giving joy to others."*
>
> —Sri Chinmoy

Go on the Date

As I tried to balance my new responsibilities at ESP with college life, the hamster wheel seemed to only speed up as I attempted to eat Waffle House at 2 a.m., attend late-night concerts, and play capture the flag on UGA's North Campus. I knew my limitations and was fully aware I could not do this alone. I had Alison to help me, but there was still another partnership I longed for. I wanted companionship, someone to talk to about the challenges, someone who could get excited about the wins. I needed someone who was thinking about me.

Okay, I wanted a husband.

While my peers focused on the traditional college experience, looking forward to their career, dating for fun, and dreaming about getting married much later, I had already begun living out my career. Marriage came next, right?

I'll never forget sitting on my IKEA platform bed, hiding from my roommate, and writing a prayer. . .for a husband.

This is stupid, I argued with myself at one point. *No one wants to find their husband this early in life.*

Culture was saying I was crazy; I was too young. It was hard to ignore that. But the spirit inside me said otherwise.

I finished my prayer. It reflected what was truly in my heart.

Two weeks later I received a phone call.

"Hey, this is Joseph," he said. "I'm driving into Athens from Atlanta and heard from Kevin that you would be a great girl to take out. Would you like to go on a date with me?"

Kevin was UGA's campus pastor. And Joseph had grown up with Kevin, which meant one thing: he was seven years older than me.

Which meant he was playing little league baseball when I was born.

I was still flattered he called, and I said yes without much more information. This was my first-ever blind date.

It's just a date, I thought. *And there is no way I'm telling my parents that I am going on a date with a geriatric patient.*

That Saturday, Joseph picked me up in his old Ford Explorer with a giant University of Florida Gator head on the rear window. First, a century older than me, and now *this*. He was in Bulldog country where football culture runs deep. And he was rolling in with an enemy mascot filling his rear window. When I saw him pulling up to meet me, I assumed a guy sporting a gray mullet and homemade jorts would step out of the vehicle; and if so, I would just run.

Instead, a tall, sandy blonde-haired man with big blue eyes stepped out. It was enough for me to temporarily forget about his allegiances.

The Blind Date

We met Kevin and his wife Elizabeth for a double date at a local pizza pub called Transmetropolitan. Little did I know how transformative the night would be. The conversation flowed easily, and afterward we went to their house to watch *Serendipity* and eat chocolate-covered strawberries.

The date was fun, easy, and enjoyable. Still, I was sure Joseph was a serial dater at his age. I was just the next girl to come along.

As he drove me back to the dorms, we finally had the opportunity to talk one-on-one. It was then I realized there was something different about Joseph. Throughout the conversation he owned his faults so openly it was as if he was influencing me to not accept a second date. It had the opposite effect. From that conversation on, I was smitten by a characteristic in him that's uncommon today—humility. It is something we often struggle to teach our kids or model ourselves because humility is often portrayed as a weakness. But in my upside-down world at ESP, this narrative is constantly challenged.

The opposite of humility is hubris, a term that derives from Greek mythology, signifying the dangerous combination of over-confidence, over-ambition, arrogance, and pride. In the Ancient Greek world, hubris was considered to be one of the most dangerous traits one could exhibit.

The truth is that I don't think anyone sets out to exhibit hubris. Most often, hubris just happens. Humility, on the other hand, must be harvested. I think of hubris as the easier path. Succeed and you get to wear the success. Be that successful person. Let people know. Hubris is about trumpeting a platform. Humility is different. It means that even when you reach the top, your posture remains grounded. Humility is about stewarding your posture in a way that doesn't set yourself above others—ever. It requires much more intentionally than accepting your due praise and keeping your celebration going.

Figure 5.1 shows the humility spectrum.

Figure 5.1 The humility spectrum

How do we learn to exercise humility in a culture that more readily rewards self-praise?

Observe those who have it in spades.

I was surrounded by such people at ESP, and now I could not help but fall for a man who displayed it with ease. Unfortunately, we often miss these teachers of humility. Maybe it's more accurate to say that we underestimate what they have to offer. But what they offer can profoundly change the way we lead, live, and love. Caleb's story is a prime example.

Look Past the Pastor

One blistering 95-degree camp afternoon, our group of 100 ESP campers splashed in the University of Georgia pool when, midway through my twentieth game of Marco Polo, I was summoned to the locker room. Caleb, a handsome, 6-foot, sports loving, 20 year old with an intellectual disability, stood there bleeding profusely from his bottom while his panicked 18-year-old counselor froze. I grabbed the shower hose, rinsed away the blood, dialed 911, and, as Caleb rocked and vocalized his fear, we rubbed his head and sang camp songs until EMTs arrived.

At the hospital intake desk minutes later, his sweat-soaked father, Vernon, rushed in, signed forms with shaking hands and then climbed into the bed to cradle Caleb and softly sing "Jesus Loves Me." I sat beside them for four hours, stroking Caleb's arm and listening to a story that I have shared again and again since hearing it that day.

When Caleb was born, a pastor told his parents that hidden sin caused their son's condition, a judgment that drove Vernon from God and into addiction, first to work, then to alcohol. This fractured his marriage and distanced him from Caleb and his daughter. Years later, alone in a hotel room and contemplating suicide, Vernon opened the bedside Bible to the Apostle John's account of the man born blind.

As the story goes, Jesus' friends asked him whose sin had made the man blind—his or his parents'. Jesus clarified that neither the man's nor his parents' sin had made him blind; he was born blind so that "the works of God might be displayed in him." In that moment, the lie Vernon had been told about Caleb was shattered. There was nothing Vernon had done to cause Caleb to be how he was. In fact, it was very much the opposite: *Caleb was the way he was so that Vernon, and others, could see.*

Vernon stood from the bed, checked out of the hotel, resigned from his job, quit drinking, and returned home to rebuild his marriage and bonds with his kids—particularly the son he never really took the time to know.

By Divine intervention, Vernon leaned *all* in. He rekindled his marriage and fell in love with a son he never knew. It was just a few years later that Vernon's wife, Caleb's mom, was killed in a car accident. But Vernon and Caleb still had each other.

As I watched him cradle his son and listened to their story, I sobbed. It was a redemption tale that I could not relate an ounce to and, yet, it gave words to what my heart already sensed about people with disabilities.

Their disabilities give us an opportunity to see Divine qualities in an unobstructed, untainted way.

It's easy to be enchanted by the confident, the proud, the rich, and the famous. Yet, I believe the secret ingredients to life that we're all searching for can be found in the young, meek, and those who appear to be weak.

I don't know what your experience with church or God or religion has been. Perhaps, it has been like Vernon's, and a hubris-driven person turned you off to it some time ago. As I sat there listening to Vernon, I was confused by churches and religion too. But it was in that moment, watching a dad cradle his adult son, that I was reminded how easily hubris happens. Even Jesus' friends assumed the blind man deserved his plight. In assuming this, they were making another assumption they hadn't considered: they were better than him. More worthy. But Jesus' words woke them up to the truth: others' worth isn't physical or mental; God works in an upside-down way, and worth is found internal.

Eat the Pie

During the time I knew Caleb, there was a coffee shop downtown my friends and I loved to study at called Hot Corner. It had decent coffee, grungy couches, and delicious pie. One of my best friends was a pie aficionado. Her family's apple pie recipe had been passed down for generations with a secret ingredient. And she *loved* the pie they served at Hot Corner. We thought it might have the same secret ingredient.

We continued to whittle our college late nights away at Hot Corner, until my same friend's parents began going through a tumultuous divorce. Her depression that followed made it difficult to leave her apartment.

I decided one day to head to Hot Corner and spend whatever it took to get her a whole apple pie. She deserved it. I walked up to the counter but did not see a pie in the case.

"Excuse me, I'd like to buy one of your apple pies," I said, assuming there was more in the back. There was never *not* apple pie at Hot Corner.

The barista with thick-framed glasses, scrappy hair, and a scruffy beard looked at me and then the case. "Uh, we are out," he said. "But you can head to Sam's Club and get one if you want. That's where we buy them."

The pie. That my pie connoisseur bestie adored. That we assumed had some secret ingredient. Was $5.98 at Sam's Club.

Many of us try to be like that Hot Corner apple pie. We craft a persona and a supporting narrative to let others know that we are special and worthy of their time and attention. We forget that what ultimately makes us worthy is not the presentation. It's what's inside us and the impact that has on others.

Let It Lead

I ended up marrying that guy from the blind date. I trusted him more than any other guy I had dated because I could see what was on the inside of him from the very beginning. It took humility on his part to share it, but what that led to was a profound connection that changed both of our lives forever.

Our wedding was on the eve of New Year's Eve in downtown Atlanta. The candlelight, the light rain, and the 300 people who joined us made for a winter whimsy of an evening. But what everyone who was there remembers about our wedding is not when I walked down the aisle. They remember the moment right before that.

Megan and Dakota, two of my ESP favorites, served as a flower girl and a ring bearer. Megan is a hilarious brunette who loves to yell, "Thank you, Jesus!" and regularly greets ladies with, "Hey, Diva!" She was born with a rare chromosomal deletion. Her job was to join my four future nieces in sprinkling flower petals down the aisle before I made my entrance. Dakota is a blonde-haired, blue-eyed stunner with a passion for sports. He was born with cerebral palsy. Dakota's job was to wheel himself down the aisle while ringing a bell and announcing the bride.

He nailed the rehearsals and was so excited about his job. But when the big day came and the music started playing, he froze at the end of the aisle. All eyes on him. Everyone began wondering the same thing. . .should we do something?

Just then, unplanned, two of my bridesmaids, one of them Alison, walked back up the aisle to Dakota. One pushed his wheelchair down the aisle as the other rang the bell. Meanwhile, Dakota smiled bright and yelled, "The bride is coming!"

Next up, the flower girls lined up for their own debut. All five girls began walking, heeding the instruction to smile while sprinkling petals on the aisle to prepare for the bride. My four nieces followed the instructions to a T. Meanwhile Megan, excited by the limelight, took one step down the aisle and dumped her whole basket at her feet as she giggled and yelled, "So excited!"

As "You Raise Me Up" by Josh Groban began playing, my 8-year-old niece glanced back and saw Megan still standing with her pile of petals. She jogged back and reached out her hand. Together, the two strutted down the aisle as Megan giggled with excitement and anticipation.

The bride had not even entered the room and tears of joy rolled down every cheek in the building.

It was a beautiful reminder that despite our constant efforts at perfection, we are still more touched and moved by the humble, imperfect humanity in people.

Joseph watched all this transpire with tears flooding his face. This was the day he'd been waiting for his whole life, and it could not have been more perfectly imperfect. And neither he nor I would have had it any other way. I think I can say the same was true for every guest there. There was an unforgettable magic in those humble moments.

I used to think that time and experience would help me gain more credibility. I thought I needed more personal success and corporate wins to bridge the divide between my young age and professional worthiness. Even in my more defined years of leadership, I was inducted into a prestigious state-wide leadership program where, thankfully, spouses were able to join in. It was about time Joseph got to benefit from the free dinners.

After a year in the program, I began to hear a whisper that Joseph had distinguished himself among the men in our year's group with the name #LovelikeJoseph—an anthem that inspired other men, many of whom were also Leadership recipients and highly distinguished leaders throughout the state. Through his humble and gentle disposition, Joseph had quietly become a model for them.

The world applauds the loudest voice, but it's the quiet strength of humility that lingers. When you choose humility, people may not notice you first—but they may remember you longest. I've seen it in Joseph, and I've seen it in our members at ESP—in the way they instinctively put others first, giving joy to others and creating a kind of oneness you can feel the moment you walk into the room.

I thought my blind date was with a man. But in reality, it was with humility itself—the quiet, steady kind that sneaks in, changes the temperature of a room, and stays for a lifetime.

Humility costs nothing, but it can change everything.

CHAPTER 6

The Hulk

What Happens When We Exchange Empathy for Compassion?

> *"Being unwanted, unloved, uncared for, forgotten by everybody—I think that is a much greater hunger, a much greater poverty than the person who has nothing to eat."*
> —Mother Teresa

Feel the Rub

Sweat rolled down my face. Summer in Georgia with a broken air conditioning unit and 60 bodies stuffed in a small building was brutal. But the first week of camp had arrived along with the annual camp cologne: body odor plus peanut butter and jelly sandwiches plus chlorine.

I sat in my closet-sized office trying to temporarily filter out the sounds of potential behavior problems in the gym. I needed to find a way to allow more kids to come to camp. We'd already started a waitlist, and it was growing. For some organizations, this high demand would be a big win. I didn't see it this way. I saw demand without supply as needs not being met. A waitlist for ESP Summer Camp was not the same as the years-long waitlist to become a UGA season ticket holder.

I sat with my Chaco sandals covered in mud from the morning's activity, answering one phone call after the next. Some parents were requesting more weeks for their child at camp, while others were checking on their special needs child currently at camp. But sprinkled in were calls from new families who had heard of this remarkable place called ESP. As I fielded the calls with the phone on one shoulder, I tried to review the upcoming bowling schedule sitting in front of me on my desk. Meanwhile, the bus driver was staring at me to sign her paycheck.

Lord have mercy—I forgot to finish the bus drivers' checks.

I paused, signed quickly, and mouthed sorry.

Back to the mother on the phone. She sounded desperate. She had not slept through the night in 10 years. Her daughter with autism needed a place, and she needed the space to breathe. Her marriage was unraveling. I did my best to take enough notes to remember their situation.

"Welcome to the family," I told her as we finished the call. "I'll put you on the waitlist, and if anything becomes available this summer, I'll let you know right away."

She sounded relieved and hopeful. I still felt for her. I hoped that we'd somehow end up with space for her daughter, but I knew it would likely not happen.

The waitlist had multiplied as summer approached, and our 1,200-square-foot building could not hold one more sweaty body. What began as a list of a few names and phone numbers on waitlist scratch paper turned into a scrollable Excel spreadsheet.

As the bus driver walked out, I peered out my single window to see the kids playing with energetic college counselors. There were so many smiles, which warmed my heart, particularly the crazy, bright-eyed smile of Goon. I looked around for his sidekick, the Hulk, but I didn't see him. Then I remembered we didn't have room for him that week.

Goon and the Hulk were the best of friends. I had squeezed them both in for two weeks, but only one of them was together. This was the week they were apart. Goon was there without him. He was a tall, lanky 18-year-old with freckles, googly eyes, and a contagious crooked smile. He was the resident comedian, loved giving our college counselors a hard time, enjoyed making up nicknames, and ate five bologna sandwiches for lunch every day. He also had an intellectual delay but would still strategically sneak a kiss on a girl's cheek any chance he got. His name was obviously not Goon, but it's what he called himself. So we went with it.

His right-hand man was the Hulk. At a stocky 4 feet tall with dark hair, squinty eyes, and thick lips, with Down syndrome, he was the perfect superhero complement to Goon. He'd walk through our doors each day of camp with no words, only a full Hulk stance with muscles flexed. He'd then add a bonus booty shake.

Goon and the Hulk were the sweetest pair. They didn't talk much but still operated in perfect synchronicity through their shenanigans. In the week of camp in which they'd been together, Hulk laughed at all of Goon's jokes, and Goon had a way of making the Hulk feel seen. In one of many talent shows, Goon and the Hulk showed their skills in a wrestling match. Goon, tall and slim, contorted in every direction and continued to figure out a way to dominate the Hulk...until the very end when Goon let the Hulk take out his long legs. The Hulk then stood on Goon's back proudly, muscles drawn, eyes squinted, and flashed a huge smile. The whole camp went wild.

Goon and the Hulk came alive at ESP. My only wish was that I could find space to get them in camp together for more than one week. With the long waitlist ahead of them and our limited space, it didn't look likely. But I kept trying.

Get Angry

The days ran by quickly that summer until one scorching Wednesday of Goon's week in camp without his hulking partner.

I'd already done what I did every day: led a pep rally for the staff, joined the welcome wagon for the campers, passed out medications, signed paychecks, planned the upcoming days, and took or returned parent phone calls.

I had just finished talking to a new parent when another call came in. A sheriff was on the other line from a rural, neighboring county. I couldn't quite hear him, so I hopped out of my chair, leaving a wet bathing suit stain behind, and closed the door, trying to drown out the busy camp noise.

"I am so sorry to share this with you," he then said, "but one of your campers has died."

My mind raced through who it could have been—the medically fragile ones, the ones who had recently been sick. A few names went through my head. Who could he be talking about? Then he shared the camper's name.

He was talking about the Hulk.

He was on the waiting list for camp that week. There wasn't room for him and several others whose families wanted them to be there. Instead, the Hulk was at home by himself. There are no babysitting services for young adults with disabilities, and his mom had to work or she would lose her job. While she was working, the Hulk's house caught on fire. He couldn't get out in time. Neither his bulky stature nor his squinty smile could save him.

I hung up the phone and stared out the window of my office. I saw Goon chasing a counselor who stole one of his bologna sandwiches. Instead of smiling, all I could think was that he would never get to see his best friend again.

That moment was all it took. I already had a fire burning in me about not being able to accommodate every camper who wanted to be at ESP. Losing the Hulk under those circumstances was like lighter fluid on the fire of my soul.

We had to get rid of the waiting list. I had to get rid of the waiting list.

There were a million reasons we could not get rid of it. We were in the middle of the most significant recession in centuries, and no one was donating money. I was simply trying to make it through on the funds we had by serving the kids we could. We did not have the space for more kids. The waitlist felt like a mountain too big to climb.

I only had some of the answers. It was outside my pay grade, which, at the time, was still hourly if and when I billed it. It felt like something a now 24-year-old trying to work herself through graduate school could not accomplish. It would take hundreds of thousands of dollars to build a new building to eliminate the waiting list.

But I no longer cared. It wasn't enough to be empathetic to the families and their campers who were left out and left at home. Empathy didn't change anything.

Now I was angry. And sometimes anger is the motivator we need that moves us from empathy to action.

Flip the Tables

I remember the first time I read about when Jesus walked into a church and saw a crowd of people buying and selling goods like the place was a swap meet. This building designated for godly reverence had become a place of seedy, greedy business practices. Jesus started flipping over tables and chasing the people from the building, wearing his thoughts about them on his.

Some things in life merit our anger. In the right time and place, that anger can move us to accomplish something more than feeling another's pain.

Maybe it's time to refocus our anger away from things like slow-moving traffic or coaches who don't give our kids enough playing time and toward the hurting people who don't have the capacity or resources to help themselves.

Up until hearing about the Hulk's death, my heart hurt for the parents and kids on our waiting list. I knew we had a beautiful place where their child would be loved while the parents received the respite they needed. But feelings didn't change anything. It took the Hulk to move me into action.

Most of us hear the word empathy and consider it a positive, important trait. And it is. But empathy is a feeling. It isn't an action.

Empathy refers to the emotion you feel when you feel another's pain, sadness, or struggle. You might spot a person begging for money, or a child being ignored by his peers, or an older person struggling with their grocery bags. And your heart twinges a little. You feel sad, hurt, or even heartbroken on their behalf. You might even feel guilty you are enjoying your day or life or relationship. But those feelings don't change anything about the other person's circumstances.

Nothing changes until you act on those feelings.

According to Stanford researchers Goetz, Keltner, and Simon-Thomas, compassion is a step more than empathy. You might say compassion is emotion matched with action. It's a unique mixture of sadness and love. It blends the recognition of suffering with the desire to help one who is suffering.[1] Compassion is doing something, changing something, moving something, or holding someone.

Stanford Medicine's Center for Compassion and Altruism Research and Education has been studying compassion for the last decade. Many of their findings are shared in *The Oxford Handbook of Compassion*, in which they state: "Compassion is a specific emotional response to suffering. Empathy alone lacks a specific social urge, while compassion expressly involves feeling concerned and wanting to do something to reduce another's suffering."[2]

Being an empath is wonderful. We'd all rather have empathetic friends than apathetic ones. But what's better than being an empathetic person is being a compassionate person.

When I want to remember the important difference in being compassionate, I tell myself the word *compassion* means *come* to another person with *passion*.

Compassion, not empathy, is the lifeblood of human connection, leadership, and meaningful impact. We don't help one another, hold one another, or grow closer to one another by feeling each other's feelings. We do all of those things by acting on those feelings—even the anger that arises from circumstances that shouldn't be.

It is no coincidence that compassion is a leading indicator of success in social connections and a significant predictor of health and well-being. Even Charles Darwin, the evolutionist champion of what became known as survival of the fittest, noted at the end of his life that interdependence, not mere independence, is essential for survival.[3] While he never stated outright that interdependence is more important than independence, his mature theory—especially in *The Descent of Man*—moved increasingly toward recognizing the evolutionary significance of social bonds and active cooperation in each other's lives.

Maybe you haven't had great examples of compassion in your life. You saw your parents feel a twinge of empathy and turn the other way. Perhaps you built a cadence of turning the other way because you don't know how to do the alternative. But doing something, anything, when somebody needs help is usually better than doing nothing.

And here's the good news: you and I were born with the capacity to be compassionate toward others. Compassion has been observed in infants as young as 18 months old.[4] We have no excuse to remain in our feelings about people who could use our help.

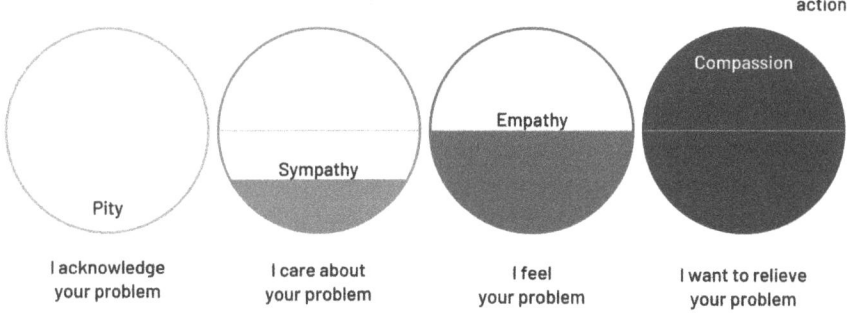

FULLFILLING COMPASSION

I wish I had taken greater measures sooner to ensure people like the Hulk never missed a day of camp. After his tragic passing, I vowed that compassion would drive me into action again and again. It was not enough for me to feel.

Flame the Spark

That summer, we had a waitlist of 100 campers. But if you think about it, we are all dealing with a waitlist. Wherever we go, there is almost always. . .

> Someone waiting for a smile
>
> Someone waiting for a friend
>
> Someone waiting for a ride

Someone waiting for encouragement

Someone waiting for a meal

Someone waiting for a family

In your class, business, church, and city, someone is always waiting for another to lean in and take action that will create positive change. Could that someone be you?

The answer is yes. But no one can turn your feelings into action but you.

The Hulk's death didn't just fuel my fire—it ignited a movement. And not just inside me. It changed everyone at ESP and many in the city of Athens. We would need everyone to do what needed to be done.

The waiting list stayed as an active tab on my computer, full of kids who wanted, needed, and deserved the magic of ESP. I saw it every time I opened my computer, and it fanned the flame of action. It pushed me to stop dreaming and start doing something. I would not stop until I could close the tab and delete the waitlist.

Regardless of the current economic condition, I had to figure out how to help more people see people of all abilities the way we saw them at ESP.

To this day, a hulk figurine remains on my bookshelf. It's a daily reminder to keep the flame inside me active—to refuse to accept empathy as a solution and instead allow compassion to compel me to either be the solution or seek the solution.

Emotion is not the same as action.

If I'd not met the Hulk, I might have never considered the critical difference. Now I will never forget it.

I hope you don't either.

Though I didn't see it right away that summer, the moment I began exchanging empathy for action at every opportunity was the moment my future, and the future of ESP, were simultaneously transformed.

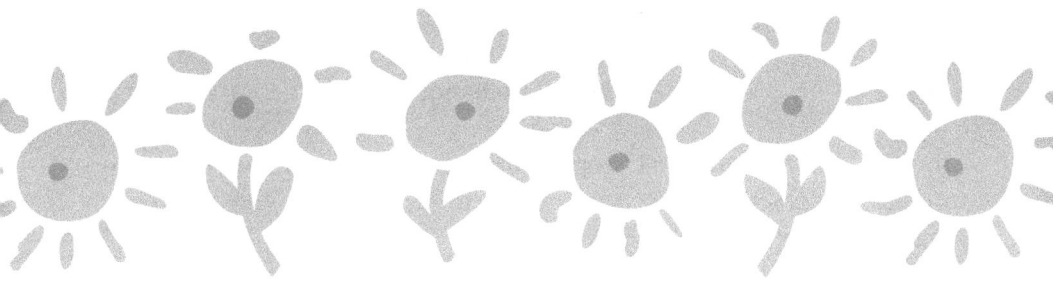

CHAPTER 7

The Flip Turn

What Happens When We Exchange Comfort for Connection?

> *"Discomfort is the price of admission to a meaningful life."*
> —Susan David

Let It Bind

My first swim buddy at camp was Mia. I taught her how to do a flip turn. A few years later, she flip turned my whole life upside down.

Mia is my age and has squinty eyes, dark skin, and an undeniable love for pizza, bowling, parties, and the Disney Channel. She also has Down syndrome. She may be a foot shorter and two times my weight, but don't let that fool you—she's absolutely weightless in the pool. Her breaststroke has earned her a wall full of Special Olympics medals.

At first, I tried to earn her friendship the way any clever camp counselor would—with snacks. It worked. Yet, after one half-hour in the water, we had invented a game we called "lifesaver." I would swim to the deep end and pretend to drown, and Mia would scoop me up and yell, "Swim buddy, I save you!" The lifeguards weren't thrilled, but we couldn't stop laughing. From that moment on, an unlikely friendship was built, and she would carry me—in more ways than I could understand.

Mia could only swim during the summer because there were no programs throughout the year. Like many individuals with disabilities, she wrestled with both physical health and a deep need for social connection. A few hours a week or a once-a-year Special Olympics meet wasn't enough. She needed rhythm. Connection. And so did Ruthie, and her best buddy Trey, and his best friend Richie.

That kind of connection takes effort. And effort is uncomfortable.

But discomfort was never something my friends at ESP saw as a problem, so we started a swim team with the only person I knew who could do it: my little sister.

My sister, then a freshman at UGA, didn't know how to run a swim team for athletes with special needs—but she knew swimming as an avid high school swimming athlete. So she took what was familiar, what she could do in her sleep, and bravely stretched it into unfamiliar territory. And thank goodness she did.

The ESP Piranhas began practicing twice a week, building not just skill but confidence. By the time the Special Olympics rolled around, they were unstoppable. While most teams only trained for the competition, our swimmers had rhythm, endurance, and flip turns sharp enough to leave waves behind. They brought home a sea of gold medals.

Swimming is inherently uncomfortable—tight bathing suits, freezing water, rubber caps that squeeze your head. And then you add spectators. And disability. And insecurity. And yet despite the uncomfortability, camaraderie can still flow in abundance. Our swimmers found strength, confidence, and connection on the other side of all the discomfort.

That's what discomfort does—either it binds us up or it binds us together.

Let's Do It

After our first summer together, Mia was there through all my big life transitions.

The Flip Turn

I found out I was pregnant in the middle of graduate school, running ESP, newly married, and utterly exhausted. Joseph and I lived in a tiny apartment and were barely scraping by. He was in school too, working two hourly jobs to keep the lights on.

Most of the time.

One evening, our power was cut off. I was studying for exams and prepping for the Special Olympics swim meet. I grabbed a flashlight and continued. When dinner time was approaching, I remember standing in the dark kitchen thinking: *I can be angry. . .or I can make food by candlelight.*

I chose the latter. It felt like survival and grace wrapped into one.

That season of life was full of small decisions like that—daily flip turns of discomfort. Joseph and I were in what I call the "gut-wrenching grocery" phase of life. If you've never lived through this, let me explain:

> You shop with anxiety sitting on your shoulders. You add items to your cart—only the essentials—and still find yourself rearranging everything on the conveyor belt, from most important to least.
>
> When it's your turn to check out, you hold your breath. You try to act calm, but your palms are sweaty, and your eyes are doing silent math, watching every beep of the scanner. You begin to hope that maybe the Lucky Charms won't scan, or maybe they'll go on sale mid-ring.
>
> And then, quietly, humbly, with the line behind you growing and your face burning, you say to the cashier: "I'm actually going to take that off. And those too."
>
> You watch her void the marshmallow cereal and the extra things you know your pregnant body is craving. When you finally step outside, grocery bags lighter than you hoped, you cry in the car. Because of the cereal, yes, but also because of the weight of trying to hold it all together.

I had never experienced that kind of discomfort before. I grew up with cereal privilege—pantries that were always full, choices that were always available. That moment was a turning point for me.

It stripped away any illusion of control and gave me eyes to see how many others walk through life silently carrying the same weight.

It was in that season that Mia's mom approached us.

Her family situation was changing, and Mia needed a place to live—and someone to help care for her. Mia's mom offered to pay us for in-home hours if we were willing to open our home.

I went to Joseph—who was already carrying the load of accounting school, multiple jobs, fatherhood, and a wife mid-meltdown—and I asked him: "What if Mia came to live with us?"

He paused. Thought. And then I watched the weight on his shoulders shift, perhaps lighten. This was not from the idea of more work, but from the memory of his own family's flip turn.

His father, a district attorney, once mentored a young boy with a rough home life. At the age of eight, Joseph's parents adopted the boy, moving Joseph from oldest child to the middle child. That boy—Chris—is now part of our family story. He's a living example of what can happen when you step into discomfort and choose love.

Joseph looked at me and said, "I think that could be really great for everyone. Let's do it."

And so we did.

We found a slightly bigger rental and added Mia to our family.

It was uncomfortable.

It was unpredictable.

And it was exactly what we needed.

She brought comedic relief, party planning, cake demands, and birthday countdowns. She never missed a celebration and taught my children to value the small joys in life: a haircut, a shared laugh, a familiar birthday meal. She became their Aunt Mia—stashing Little Debbies under the couch cushions and always up for a Disney marathon.

Over the years, she was woven into every layer of our family. When I was pregnant with our second, Mia told everyone the baby would be born on the due date, October 1. We tried to tell her that often was not the case. But Finley Gray Whitaker arrived right on time, as Mia had predicted. And when our third child was due near Mia's own birthday, she made clear that he would *not* arrive on October 19. Naturally, I went into labor the night of her party. Tate was born at 2 a.m. on October 20. The pink icing remained hers alone.

Our family photo looked different. Strangers would ask my children, "Who is that?" Their answer gave us a chance to talk about love and family friendship. Mia was a daily reminder that the life we imagined is rarely as rich as the life we allow to unfold.

After 15 years in our home, Mia eventually moved into her own apartment—just a half-mile down the road. I still see her often. But I still see daily the ripple of what she added to our lives: perspective, presence, and the courage to challenge discomfort.

Push Off the Wall

The beauty of a flip turn is that just as you're tiring from one lap in one direction, you tuck, turn, and push off the wall—gaining momentum in a new direction.

In relationships, discomfort is inevitable. But when we lean into it instead of backing away, we create space for a level of connection that often surprises us. Not only do we discover new friends, we discover a joy in friendship that isn't possible when we play it safe and simply relate to those we already know.

Discomfort often invites us to choose between retreat and relationship. I've found that when we choose relationship, we find people we never knew we needed. And we discover that the lack of comfort isn't pain—it's beautiful possibility.

Discomfort is not the enemy. It's the invitation.

When I look back at the flip turns in my life—the literal ones in the pool and the figurative ones in grocery store lines, late-night conversations, and shared meals with Mia—I see a clear pattern: discomfort came first. Then awkwardness, fear, difference, even loneliness. But instead of turning away, we pushed off the wall and turned toward one another.

It wasn't always easy. Friendship, especially with someone different from you, demands humility, patience, and a willingness to fumble your way through. But it also holds the power to transform a life—sometimes your own.

The U.S. Surgeon General recently issued an advisory on what he calls our "epidemic of loneliness." He writes that disconnection doesn't just hurt our hearts; it harms our bodies. The health risks of social isolation are comparable to smoking 15 cigarettes a day. It increases the risk of depression, anxiety, heart disease, stroke, and even premature death.

But here's the hopeful part: even small steps toward connection, toward community, can reverse that risk. And often, those steps are uncomfortable. They ask us to host the dinner, have the hard conversation, or say yes to a new friend we don't yet understand.

That's what Mia taught me. Our relationship didn't start in perfect ease; it started in the deep end—with pool goggles, snack bribes, and unsure steps. And from that discomfort grew something deeper than friendship. She became family. She changed the shape of my days and the way I define friendship and how I celebrate birthdays.

Meaningful connection is rarely smooth and straightforward; it shows up in unexpected places at unexpected times with unexpected questions. And the question it always asks first is whether you're willing to confront discomfort to discover the relational joy that lies beyond it.

In a culture that urges you to crave comfort, I encourage you to crave something far better. When relational discomfort confronts you, don't back down. Instead, push against its wall and watch the momentum of choosing connection bless you in ways you never knew you needed.

You might just find your family there.

SECTION TWO

From Invisible to Invaluable

By this point in the book, I hope you are beginning to shift your perspective on those around you—the people you least expect who can illuminate some of life's greatest lessons.

You have likely had the common childhood experience of picking the bright yellow dandelion, shining in golden sunlight, or choosing one in seed form to make the perfect childhood wish. But this common experience somehow flips into the adult narrative, as this same iconic flower becomes a weed.

I remember overhearing one of my 60-year-old neighbors talk about another neighbor's overgrown yard. The next day, I walked with my daughter, and as we passed the overgrown yard, she exclaimed, "Mommy! Look at all the beautiful flowers that are growing. Let's make some wishes!"

My daughter saw something different than my adult neighbor. They valued different things.

And while I am a fan of manicured lawns, it was a reminder that what we choose to see matters—it changes how we navigate life and interact with others and the narratives we hold within ourselves.

As we have recognized, culture does this to us. It changes what we think about things and people. Our experiences and what has been modeled determine if we have leaned in or chosen to walk by. Our minds form patterns on how we see the world. When you begin to see things from a new perspective, the narrative changes, and so do we.

Inside the "weed" is the little yellow flower that brought light to us as children. Inside the little yellow flowers are nutrients providing numerous health benefits. And those nutrients are relied upon by the bees, who use them in the first part of spring to pollinate everything.

When you are out in your yard or when you stop at a stoplight and look to see a median full of them or when you go on a walk, you may begin to see them differently, because we have brought a new perspective.

New perspectives change how you interact with the world and with others. When we begin to see the unseen and unearth the often invisible is when we truly start to see what is truly invaluable.

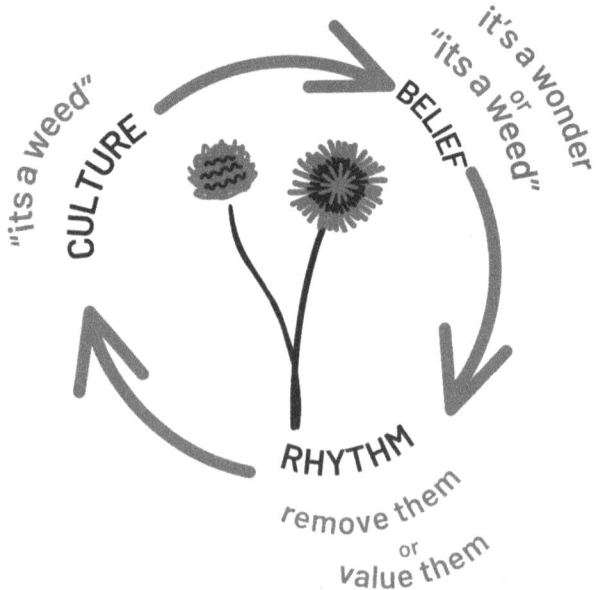

CHAPTER 8

The Hope Cup

What Happens When We Exchange Hard for Hope?

> *"Hope is being able to see the light, despite all the darkness."*
> —Archbishop Desmond Tutu

Own the Reality

I kept dreaming about a building beautiful enough to hold ESP's joy and big enough to match our heart. In the dream, there was sunlight and space and room for every name on the waitlist.

In reality, I unlocked the door to our recently donated "additional space" and found little brown nuggets scattered across dented desks and a rusted mini-fridge. We called them "chocolate sprinkles" so we didn't have to say what they really were.

Rat poop.

The air held a permanent hint of bleach. The roof leaked into a bucket we emptied more often than we wanted to admit. Two-stall bathrooms doubled as changing rooms; we spread pool mats on the floor to lift adults out of their chairs and change them on the floor with as much dignity as we could.

New families would call, breathless with what they'd heard: the laughter, the friendships, the life-changing days. All of it true. Then they would arrive, step into our space, and I'd watch a subtle shift cross their faces—the very human effort to reconcile excellence with surroundings that did not yet match it.

I wasn't ashamed of our work. The opposite. The work made me ache for a place as worthy as the people inside it. The waitlist kept growing. The dream in my head stopped feeling optional and started feeling necessary.

Find the Right Power

The tall one found us through his wife, an occupational therapist. Her patients lit up when they talked about ESP. Later, when his dad began a family foundation, he and his wife showed up at our door with their two little boys and asked to volunteer.

I was in over my Chacos with meds and payroll, so I gave them a job. They stayed the whole day and reappeared at dismissal—one boy dripping from water battles, the other with peanut butter in his hair. This suburban family had leaned all the way into a day at summer camp with kids with disabilities—and they'd never looked happier.

"We'll be back tomorrow," they said.

The next day, they dropped a $20,000 check on my desk.

They became dear friends and then board members—joining a parent-run group already fueled by a fierce, daily love. Our board looked like our community: schoolteachers and parents, a banker who taught me spreadsheets, a university professor, and a few more moms and dads who wanted their children to have more than the world had offered so far.

We were a motley bunch—long on heart, short on resources.

That summer, in the middle of a Georgia monsoon, we gathered next door to our leaky building for a board meeting. I began with the why: the names on the waitlist, the reality of our space, and the Hulk-size hole driving me now. I painted the picture of what could happen if we dared to exchange all this hard for hope.

Heads lifted. Pens started scribbling. Ideas hit the whiteboard like popcorn.

Then—dark.

The power cut out with a thunk.

I sprinted through the rain to the boys' sleepover, braced for chaos: campers with Down syndrome panicking in the dark, boys on the spectrum overwhelmed by the sudden shift, a roof bucket overflowing into a lake. The bucket was indeed overflowing, but the boys were fine—flashlights in hand, fully engaged in a smelly, rollicking game of flashlight tag.

I emptied the bucket. They booed me for interrupting their boys-only party with my perfume and estrogen presence. I grinned and dashed back through the storm.

In the boardroom, a single emergency light poured a circle of glow across the whiteboard. Fifteen people sat in the half-dark, still dreaming. When we finally left, we had no electricity and somehow more power than when we came in.

We walked out with a plan. And a word.

Hope.

Know What Hope Is

People sometimes use hope like a Hallmark word—soft, fragile, fingers crossed. That kind of hope waits for the forecast to change. But the hope my life keeps teaching me is different.

When I was little, my best friend's name was also Laura, so adults used my middle name to tell us apart. I was Laura Hope. I used to think it was sweet. Now I understand it was prophetic. In this chapter of my life, hope stopped being a label and became a discipline.

A friend had told me once, "Hope isn't a strategy." She meant the passive kind, the kind that wishes. But John Parsi and Crystal Bryce at Arizona State University have studied hope for years and found it's not the same as optimism. Optimism believes things will probably turn out fine. Hope acts so they can. "Hope requires a person to take responsibility for their wants and desires and take action in working towards them," Parsi says.[1]

Optimism waits for a happy ending. Hope knocks on doors. If no one answers, it moves to the next one.

I like to picture it this way: if life were a cup, optimism says, "I hope it gets filled." Hope says, "I can see it full—now how do we fill it?"

Jeremy Webber at the U.S. Army War College pushes back on the idea that hope is fluffy. He traces some of America's greatest achievements to one stubborn ingredient: hope. Plans alone don't inspire people; hope does—both the spark at the start and the fuel to see it through.

That night, in a powerless room, we decided to put hope to work.

Ask the Marine

We needed someone who could take that fragile outline in my head and give it form. Someone who wouldn't be scared off by a bucket or a waitlist. One name kept coming up.

Toni. Petite. Perfectly put together. Marine sergeant. Accountant. Accounting professor. Two-time cancer survivor. Single mother of four, one of them Samantha, who has cerebral palsy. On paper, formidable. In person, a force.

We met at Mama's Boy, the Athens staple known for biscuits as big as your hand. I told her about the waitlist. About the families who couldn't afford private care. About the magic that happens when people who've been invisible are given a place to belong.

She listened and then looked me squarely in the eyes. "I can afford to have my daughter cared for. I know many cannot. I'd love to help them."

I also knew—because it keeps happening—that if she stepped in, the joy wouldn't be "for other people's kids" for long. It would find its way to her kitchen table, too.

A week later she called, voice urgent and bright. "Laura, Samantha just said, 'Oh my God.'" My stomach sank, misreading her tone. *There goes my force.*

Then she laughed. "No, listen—10 years of speech therapy, and she has never strung three words together. I was at the sink; she was beside me in her chair; I must have said something she didn't like. She rolled her eyes and said, 'Oh my God.' Laura, that's the most appropriate thing she's ever said!"

One week of camp had cracked open a door a decade of appointments hadn't. Supporter became champion. Toni had helped build 10 buildings for a private school. Now she wanted to build one for ESP—for Samantha, for the kids on the waitlist, and for the families who needed more than care. They needed community.

She also knew what hope needs: a picture.

Get It on Paper

Toni texted a name: Peter. "He can draw the future so people can see it."

We met in a downtown coffee shop where the smell hits you before the door closes. He sat by the window with a legal pad and a sharpened pencil, calm in that way people are when they don't need to prove a thing.

I talked, not about square footage but about people. Parents crying in my office because there was nowhere else for their child. A teenager who might speak for the first time. The way ESP makes invisible things visible.

Peter drew. His pencil moved like it already knew where we were going.

The entrance widened into a welcome area shaped like open arms. Hallways stretched wide enough for two wheelchairs to pass without apology. Sunlight spilled across floors. Rooms unfurled:

- An art room that overflows with color
- An amphitheater for gatherings and dance parties
- A parent lounges to sit and listen to laughter while nervous hearts soften
- Sensory rooms—quiet, safe, reset spaces
- A teaching kitchen for skills and for family dinners where everyone belongs
- Outdoor spaces to sing until the sun goes down
- Electronic changing tables to keep staff backs strong and the dignity of our adults intact

"Could we add a tree at the entrance?" I asked.

He drew limbs reaching up. "Why a tree?"

"Because I once read, 'Hope deferred makes the heart sick, but a hope fulfilled is a tree of life.' I want it there for every family who felt sick with deferred hope—so when they walk in, they feel the fulfillment."

We walked out with a masterpiece. It wasn't da Vinci or Monet, but it did the same quiet magic: it let people see what had existed only in our heads. Sometimes the first act of hope is a pencil moving across paper.

Fill the Cup

Now we needed more eyes. We needed a room that could hold the dream and reflect it back.

A year earlier, the Georgia Theatre had burned down. Its loss broke our city's heart; its rebuild rallied us. Could that same stage hold a different rising?

"You can't put tables and chairs on a slanted floor," the owners warned.

"Can we try?" I asked.

They said yes, part curiosity, part kindness.

We mailed 300 invitations with the names of hosts people respected—Coach Vince Dooley and his wife Barbara, sportscaster Chuck Dowdle, and others who believed enough to lend their names. I pictured a flood.

Thirty people RSVP'd yes.

We borrowed tables, borrowed cloths, and cut flowers from a friend's garden. We set for 100 and spread them out so the room looked full. We prayed for open doors.

At noon, I stood on the stage as we began. The lights blinded me. "Hope is seeing light despite the darkness," I reminded myself. Then the house lights dimmed, and the crowd came into view: more than 250 people, balcony to floor. Not a single empty seat.

We played a video a board member created: six ESP friends at camp, then walking to the theater, then opening its curtains to reveal a stage where they shared their dreams. The music built. The screen rose. The curtains parted. And there they were, our six, holding posters:

Because of ESP I can. . .play sports. Find friends. Go to camp. Be a ballerina.

One poster leaned crooked. Another was upside down. It didn't matter. The room stood. Smiled. Cried.

Toni closed with the truth every parent thinks but rarely says aloud. "When I pray at night, I do not pray for my daughter. I pray for one day when I am gone and she outlives me. I am praying for all of you—that your hearts will be open to those who are different. Will you speak up for our children who cannot speak for themselves?"

Toni's plea was was of hope, an empty cup and the opportunity to fill it with ESP and with her community.

People lined up to talk afterward. Many had no personal experience with disability, but they wanted to understand. Some used words like "retarded" and "handicapped" that made us wince; but we knew they simply didn't know better yet. I learned that day not to mistake ignorance for unwillingness. Given a chance to see, most people will.

That October afternoon was a spark. With every person who caught the vision, my sticky-note soup grew—names and numbers we could stir into this thing and turn scarcity into enough.

And then I waited for phones to ring off the hook.

They did not.

Sugar the Nae Naes

I expected checks. Instead, I got "reality checks."

"Oh sweetie, you cannot raise $3 million in this town."

"This town" had more nonprofits per capita than any other in the country, or so I was told.

"You didn't ask our permission to run a capital campaign."

Buried in a funding agreement was a clause I'd missed: if we launched a capital campaign during their funding period, we needed their board's approval. Was this really a thing?

Two weeks later, I walked into their boardroom with our board chair. "There's no better positioning than the truth," he whispered. "Tell them what families endure. Tell them ESP is their sole source of hope. Tell them about the waitlist."

They asked about a feasibility study. We didn't have one; we didn't have a donor base to survey.

"What if you don't raise the full amount?" they pressed.

I hadn't considered *if*. Only *how*.

"If we raise $200,000, we'll serve more," I said. "If we raise $1 million, we'll serve more. Whatever we raise, we'll shrink the waitlist, so every individual and family can experience this magic."

The Hope Cup

A man with white hair kept circling process, reminding me I had not followed it. Out of the corner of my eye I saw another—balding, kind eyes—lean forward. "If you're going to raise $3 million—and I hope you do—we may need you more than you need us. Our $30,000 is just a small fraction of that. How would it look for us to pull support when you need us most?"

Meeting over. Funding stayed. The leader side-hugged me in the hall. "Good luck, kid. Fundraising is hard work."

Days later, at a nonprofit seminar, I met the restroom confessional. Female bathrooms have always been safe rooms; this one reminded me they can be echo chambers too. I sat in a stall and heard my name.

"Any funds they raise will take away funds from us. They won't do it."

I waited to flush until they left. If only it were that easy to flush words from your mind. That day I learned how philanthropy can behave when scarcity is steering: competition over collaboration. It gave me something else, too—the resolve to change my mental playlist.

Remember the Whip and Nae Nae? Ray does. Ray is a 17-year-old with dark skin, a bright smile, and the coolest haircut. He also has Down syndrome. He has rhythm that can pull a camp of 100 people into the dance like it's still 2015.

We had Nae Nae naysayers, and they were whipping me back and forth until I started to believe them. If I wasn't careful, they'd break my legs.

I began with a mountain of faith, but "can't" and "won't" loosen boulders. If I wasn't careful, the avalanche would bury the very people I wanted to serve.

I value advice, but as I listened, I saw the pattern: I was surrounding myself with people who thought small, acted small, and lived in a scarcity mindset. If I wanted wisdom, I had to widen my circle, learn new dance moves, and change the station on my mental Spotify. It was time to stop replaying the same Nae Nae on repeat and start learning a whole new routine—one where hope wasn't just a feeling but the lead step.

It was time to change the playlist.

Find a New Formation

I once read about a Roman battle strategy—the testudo, the tortoise formation. Soldiers interlocked shields overhead and on all sides, advancing as one almost-impenetrable shell. Alone, a soldier was vulnerable; together, they moved.

I needed a turtle.

I thought about the balding man with the kind smile. He understood something that the others did not. He saw something the others could not see. He was dancing to a different song.

I called the kind-eyed businessman from the meeting and asked him to mentor me. Over time I learned the weight his eyes had carried: I met him as a successful businessman who bought and sold large manufacturing plants nationwide. But his kind eyes and smile of faith were not manufactured. He had three beautiful boys, one of whom was diagnosed with cancer in high school. No amount of resources could change the sheer heartache of his family. He watched his son suffer, move to a wheelchair, navigate the inaccessible world we live in, and ultimately fight until his final day. He endured his other two sons' grief and his beautiful bride, with a soul as a sunflower, losing her son. And all of this, albeit an incomprehensible challenge, strengthened his faith in what is unseen, in the hope of heaven and his goal here on earth: to love those who love those.

Trials grow perseverance. Perseverance grows a hope that lacks nothing. He didn't say that; he lived it. He signs his texts with a turtle emoji. He became the first member of my tortoise formation—people who protect you from small thinking, call you toward the larger story, and remind you that abundance is a truer song.

I started paying attention to who spoke life and who siphoned it. Who saw the cup half-empty, who just hoped it would fill, and who would join in filling it. Who saw people with disabilities as a drain and who saw them as a gift. Who believed communities could stretch and who believed they were already tapped out. I moved my chair accordingly.

Get to 90%

I began writing to major Georgia foundations. I didn't know many required an invitation to apply. We didn't have relationships to win an invitation. I mailed the letters anyway.

One evening I stirred macaroni and peas for Owen before a Chamber event and heard a voicemail: "Laura, this is John from the foundation. Please call me this evening."

My heart pounded. I called. He asked thoughtful questions. He didn't rush. And then he said, "This sounds like an amazing mission—one we'd like to be part of one day. Call me when you're 90 percent to your goal and you can submit a full proposal."

Ninety percent. Of three million. $2.7 million.

Strangely, it didn't deflate me. It moved the goalpost in my mind. He had just placed himself on our future team. Hope is social; it moves in relationships. We'll get there, I thought, and then we'll call you back.

Had it not been for the naysayers, I might've stayed local, knocking the same few doors. Their skepticism pushed me to widen the circle and refine the message. My corner grew: our board, my family, the turtle mentor, generous strangers who became friends. Hope caught like kindling.

But to get to 90 percent, we would have to move past the doubters, build real momentum at home, and rally far more people inside our own area code. My plan? Take our Georgia Theatre concept and multiply it by 10. We needed a new song—one our whole community could dance to.

Hope doesn't wait for perfect conditions; it moves with what it has. If your cup feels empty, begin by imagining it full. Find the people willing to hold it with you. And then—one knock, one sketch, one "yes" at a time—start to pour. Hope isn't just a strategy; it's the strategy that turns the invisible into the invaluable (see Figure 8.1).

Figure 8.1 The hope strategy

CHAPTER 9

The Stage

What Happens When We Exchange Power for Perspective?

> *"By adopting a certain physical posture, a resonant chord is struck in spirit."*
>
> —Bruce Lee

Feel the Cringe

I didn't know it then, but the most cringeworthy pageant I'd ever seen would lead to ESP raising millions of dollars and change how an entire community saw people with disabilities.

It began with a bad night.

I sat in a high-school auditorium two hours from home, cheering for one of our ESP campers who was part of a beauty pageant put on by some local families. The idea of a pageant for people with special needs wasn't wrong; the execution was. The music droned. The sashes looked like they'd snap if folded. The crowns were straight out of Burger King. Most painful of all, the hosts didn't know the kids on stage. The room felt timid—40 people scattered across rows, clapping politely, not sure what they were watching.

As the applause died, my heart did not. Even in that awkwardness, I could see something true: the concept had power. If we built an event that matched our people—joyful, dignified, personal—it could become a stage where the invisible turn invaluable right before our eyes.

"A...Special...Needs...Pageant?"

I pitched the idea to our board in a room that had seen better days—metal chairs, art-stained folding tables, surfaces bowed from years of use.

"A special needs pageant?" they repeated, as if they'd misheard.

"A...special...needs...pageant," I said.

"With crowns and sashes?"

"With crowns and sashes."

Silence. Then the questions tumbled out.

"Who will come?"

"What if people stare?"

"How is this not a spectacle?"

One mom—we'll call her Diane—crossed her arms and pressed the question beneath all the questions. "Laura, my daughter has autism. People stare because she acts differently. I will not have her be a spectacle."

I understood. There's an important conversation about not reducing people to their differences. But I also knew what we saw at ESP every day: ability worth celebrating, joy worth sharing, a love that does not need translation. What if we shifted the frame so the world saw what we see? Something like *American Idol* or *America's Got Talent*—but for people the world rarely spotlights—crafted not as pity but as honor.

The room split down the middle. We had little money to risk on a fundraiser no one could picture. As one with a vote, I held the tie-breaker. I thought of the waitlist, the Hulk who never got back to camp, the way a community's heart can widen when given a doorway. I voted yes. If it failed, the blame would be mine.

We named it Big Hearts and started where we could: a flyer. Microsoft Word became a cautionary tale—clashing fonts, tragic clip art, spacing that made no sense. I printed stacks at the neighborhood copy shop (one of our first "sticky-note" donors) and plastered coffee shops, clinics, and any window without a "No Soliciting" sign (and, if we're honest, a few with one).

We begged the local paper to run a story about our city's first special-needs pageant. Then we planned. And prayed.

Make It Visible

On the day of the first Big Hearts, I peeked from behind the red curtain in heels, holding my breath. I worried only a handful would come—loyal families, a few friends, maybe a gracious neighbor. You'd think I would have learned after the Georgia Theatre surprise. My worry was wrong. Nearly 250 people filled the seats.

We had promised something different—spectacular because our people are spectacular. The evening was set: a silent auction in the lobby, college staff serving as escorts, #lovelikejoseph as co-emcee with two rowdy former summer staff. The men wore tuxedos. The women wore sequins. Backstage, teen buddies had rehearsed each partner's moment to shine. Twenty contestants. One borrowed high-school stage. A mix of pageantry and celebration.

One contestant rolled in with a striking purple wheelchair. Her name was Rosie. Long brown hair. Eyes that smiled. Bedazzled shoes. And nonverbal. Her mother told us Rosie had never been far from her side. A typical pregnancy had snapped into trauma; months in the NICU had taught her parents how to manage a G-tube, how to resuscitate if she stopped breathing, how to call 911—then sent them home to figure out the rest.

At rehearsal, her mom hovered and then did the bravest thing she'd done in years: she placed Rosie's hands into the hands of a teenage buddy and sat in the audience next to her husband, eyes shining with a mix of terror and relief.

I would later share a camp cabin with Rosie and her mom. One night I woke to the sound of Rosie "talking"—groans, squeals, screeches. To most, it would be noise; to her mother it was a concert of beautiful conversation. I lay there as she answered back with tenderness and humor, fluent in a language love had taught her to hear. Words are only one way we speak. That night I learned again what our culture forgets: people who don't use words still have plenty to say.

The show itself was low-tech and high-heart. The music was loud and clean—the kind that makes you clap without thinking. Our crowd fillers modeled how to cheer with abandon. A child with Down syndrome sang "Jesus Loves You" and the room cried. An adult with cerebral palsy sank a basket and the room erupted. Rosie rolled out sparkling, and #lovelikejoseph kissed her cheek. We laughed. We cried. We saw.

Afterward, moms and dads, teachers, and grandparents lined up at the foot of the stage, tears cutting clear lines through their makeup. "My favorite night of the year," they kept saying. Even Diane—the skeptic—was beaming. Her daughter had done a ballerina twirl. The audience roared. For the first time, Diane felt the public saw her daughter's abilities.

There's a difference between seeing someone and someone being seen. Big Hearts gave parents who often felt invisible the chance to watch their child stand in the spotlight and be celebrated for the goodness they bring.

We had found a classroom large enough to retrain a community's eyes.

Give It a Voice

But to teach a city to see, we needed a bigger room.

Only a few years later, we made the leap to the largest venue in town: the theater with 2,025 seats and a banquet hall for 1,000 more. That meant more than 3,000 people could encounter the waitlist in a single night. Our board stretched to approve the risk. The venue discounted. Volunteers swarmed. Professionals lent their skills. We stitched together a team the budget couldn't have bought. And even if we'd had the money to pay everyone, the team was stronger because it wasn't galvanized by compensation; it was galvanized by heart.

That January, as we were finalizing contracts, I also got a positive pregnancy test. I was 28 and thrilled, but the timing felt comically inconvenient. A few discreet bouts of morning sickness in the catering bathroom later, we pushed ahead. Parents like Rosie's navigated the complicated every day; we could do complicated for a season.

On show night, the theater was half-full—still double the high-school crowd. An automated, computer voice spoke into the darkness. A spotlight found our narrator.

Rosie.

A girl who had never spoken a word told the story through her augmentative communication device. The script wove Broadway songs and real life—our vision to serve everyone on the waitlist, to build a place where dignity is the default. The house wept openly. Rosie closed with a monologue on difference and acceptance. She didn't say a word and yet she said everything.

After the show, the banquet hall doors opened and another stage came to life. We showed the drawings Toni and Peter had pulled from our hearts to paper—wide halls, sensory rooms, a kitchen table big enough for all of us. People ate, and they saw. By the end of the night we had raised $200,000—enough to build one activity room in our future building—and, more importantly, we had given our city a vision to carry.

It was a miracle Rosie made it to her first birthday. She didn't make it to her twenty-first. But her story wasn't done. In time, her name would grace a place where miracles keep happening. When I picture that first year on the big stage, I still see her in the spotlight—changing a thousand perspectives without a spoken word—like a butterfly whose very presence shifts the air around it.

Move the Sequins

Nothing is more dichotomous than beauty queens escorting people of all abilities across a stage. Perfect. Polished. Calculated. Then disability—authentic, uncalculated, delightfully unpredictable. That's the point. We love flipping the script, inviting queens and pageant winners to escort our people. And they love it.

We also invite SEC football players—tuxedoed and grinning—bringing swagger to match the sequins. Everyone gets the same 10-minute training to show them where to walk, what to do if a member bolts (or dives into the audience), and the most important rule—nothing will go exactly as planned.

What happens next is always my favorite part. Precision meets unpredictability. Awkwardness softens into laughter. Postures change. With posture, perspective. With perspective, lives.

One of those queens was Jenna, Miss University of Georgia. She was the kind of person who could walk into a room and make you suddenly aware of every flyaway hair—not because she was unkind but because she seemed flawless. Dark hair, deep brown eyes, pink lipstick applied like a promise. A social media influencer, a soon-to-be UGA law grad, and now. . .an escort at Big Hearts.

From the start, Jenna wanted the experience to be perfect for the on-stage participants. She listened closely in training. But Big Hearts doesn't reward perfect; it rewards presence. When curveballs came, she kept saying yes—kissing cheeks, accepting faux proposals, flexing biceps, tossing footballs in heels. She came back the next year. And the next. Eventually, she landed a job in the university's athletic department, becoming the go-to person for fans with disabilities. The kids on our stage had taught her what crowns can't: move the sequins aside, kneel, and meet people eye to eye. Sometimes the most powerful thing you can do is change your posture.

Take a Knee

In football, teams take a knee when someone is hurt. It's a posture of acknowledgment: we see you.

A few years into Big Hearts, I sent a message to UGA's freshman quarterback—#11, Aaron—hoping he might elevate the night. He said yes immediately. It turned out he and his brother, Josh, had volunteered at a muscular dystrophy camp in high school. Service was already stitched into their story.

In tuxedos, with a few teammates in tow, they showed up like they belonged there—because they did. Aaron bowed to young

The Stage

ladies in wheelchairs, lowering himself to meet their gaze. He kissed the cheeks of girls with intellectual delays who longed to be treated as ladies. Josh tossed footballs to boys who dropped every pass and still walked off as champions. When the lights went up, they didn't slip out the back; they carried trash and stacked chairs.

They were hooked. Aaron came back again and again, eventually serving as master of ceremonies when we moved to the big stage. Fist bumps. Whispered encouragements. Late nights. Zero complaints. Some came to see the quarterback, but they always left seeing so much more.

One of the clearest pictures of Aaron's heart came after one of his hardest moments. The morning after a crushing loss at Auburn—43–37, with headlines sharp as knives—we were scheduled to film a video on the UGA field about our waitlist. That night after the loss, I texted him an easy out: we can reschedule.

The text bubbles instantly appeared: I will be there. I need this now more than the kids do.

He greeted each ESP friend as if he had been waiting just for them. "Hannah, you changed your hair color! I love it," he said, catching details most men take 20 years of marriage to notice. Then he knelt, eye level, present. "Clear eyes, full hearts, can't lose," Coach Taylor says in Friday Night Lights. That morning I understood: the clearer the eyes, the fuller the heart.

Before long, a tradition was born, beginning under former Bulldogs head coach Mark Richt and carried on by Kirby Smart's Georgia football team. Numbers 53, 30, and 7 joined our events. And the joy spread quickly to others on the team and coaching staff. Another tradition was also born. Aaron, Josh, and UGA legend David Pollack started an annual golf tournament that now fuels our everyday work. Big Hearts and that tournament invite thousands—many of them initially short-sighted, consumed with stats or success—to see.

Most people assume Big Hearts is about changing the audience's perspective. It is. But something greater keeps happening: the people participating in the event leave changed, too. When you kneel, something in you stands up straighter.

Bright Lights

By 2020, Big Hearts sold out the theater—2,026 tickets—for the third time. A young country artist in green bell-bottoms opened with a tribute to members we had lost too soon. As her unforgettable voice carried and their photos filled the screen—each dressed to the nines from their moments on the Big Hearts stage—tears slid down my face.

Her name was Lainey Wilson. Before the awards and stadiums, she stood on our stage singing "You Are My Sunshine"—the song woven into ESP since the beginning. We sing it at every camp ceremony, ending with clapping and that pleading line: "Please don't take my sunshine away." That night she looked out over 2,000 people—including parents whose children were no longer with us—and, in her eyes, she told them a simple truth: I see you.

Backstage she met Nick Smith, a man with a rare form of dwarfism and a personality 10 times his stature. He calls her his "Country Girlfriend." If you watch closely at her shows, or scroll her posts, you'll still see him there. Fame didn't erase the friendship; it anchored it. Lainey holds on to that to this day because it grounds her in what she never wants to lose: the reminder that life is short and the biggest gifts often come in the smallest, most unexpected packages.

Sometimes the change sparked on the stage keeps echoing long after the lights fade. Take Lily—blonde-haired, blue-eyed, luminous. She first stepped onto the Big Hearts stage as a contestant—nervous and radiant. The applause she heard wasn't polite; it was a community seeing her. Years later, she walked onto soundstages millions recognize—the sets of Netflix and Hallmark. She often says her confidence began here, in a prom gown under bright lights. This year I stood beside her again, not just as her emcee, but as her colleague, marveling at how one night of being seen can ripple into a lifetime of stepping boldly. She now uses her light to shine on others.

What the Stage Really Does

David Brooks calls ours "an age of bad generalization," where so many problems trace back to people not feeling truly seen. John Ruskin wrote, "The greatest thing a human soul ever does is to see something, and tell what it saw plainly." Talking is common. Thinking is rarer. But seeing—clear, deep, accurate—might be the rarest and most valuable skill we can develop.[1]

Big Hearts became our way to help a whole town practice that skill. And the practice turned into muscle. Today, thousands attend. Over time, millions have been raised. What began on a paint-stained folding table is now part of our fabric, intertwining ability awareness, families of people with disabilities, and neighbors who come for a good show and leave with new eyes.

But here's the deeper exchange that keeps me awake (in the best way): power for perspective. People with platforms—queens in crowns, quarterbacks in tuxes, artists in spotlights—lay down the reflex to perform and take up the posture to perceive anew: kneel, lower, notice, lift. When that exchange happens, the person in the fancy outfit is not diminished; they are completed. And the person so often overlooked is not pitied; they are prized.

I've watched a beauty queen move a stray sequin out of her eye line, bend, and see a girl's face with unfiltered tenderness. I've watched a quarterback with a bruised ego kneel on turf and listen to a friend with Down syndrome as if she were the only person in the stadium. I've watched a singer on the cusp of mega stardom lock eyes with a parent whose child is gone and sing like a prayer.

Posture first. Perspective follows. And perspective, held long enough, becomes a life.

Keep Your Light Low and Your Eyes Level

What can you do? You don't need a stage or a spotlight to practice this exchange. You already carry more platform than you think.

Change your posture, and your perspective will follow. Don't just bend to pat a child's head; kneel to meet their eyes. Don't wave from the aisle; step into the row where the quietest person is sitting. Don't grin from across the room; sit beside the neighbor who always stands alone. Then listen—really listen. Ask a question that invites a story and give it your full attention. Move aside the sequins—title, task list, hurry—and look until you actually see.

When you lower yourself to lift another, your light doesn't get smaller; it gets warmer. Your heart doesn't empty; it fills. And the people culture overlooks begin to take their rightful place: invaluable.

I was beginning to think this was the start of something good. We were on to something. And now, we just needed to keep it growing.

CHAPTER 10

The Brags

What Happens When We Exchange Inability for Ability?

> *"The privilege of a lifetime is to become who you truly are."*
> —Carl Jung

P ass the Sweet Tea

When it comes to big hearts, Dave definitely had one.

Not in the way most people imagine—no glass-tower donor suite, no country-club underwriter, no talent for our stage. Dave was a hog farmer. White hair, tattered clothes, a belt buckle that caught the sun, and a toothy grin that felt like a handshake before his hand ever lifted. He came around because of his brother, Chuck—the same board member who'd taught me QuickBooks and coached me through a presentation where the direction was "Don't cry."

When Dave heard we were squeezing kids and wheelchairs into a small building, he found us a few old, donated classroom trailers and helped park them behind the building. He didn't say much at first. He'd lean in the doorway and ask in that slow drawl, "Laura, what are you doin'?" as if I might be playing computer games instead of juggling meds, payroll, and a waitlist that hurt to look at. He'd watched Martha build ESP. He wanted to make sure we didn't lose what she started.

One afternoon he stopped by after catching wind of our new-building dream. His family had helped found the VFW club next door, where a distressed old building sagged on a few acres. Dave worried we'd sell our place and end up with a neighbor the community didn't want. I worried about leaving the heart of what Martha built. With less than an acre, we had no room to grow, but it was holy ground—beside the city park where she'd first carved out space for our kids to belong.

"Laura, I just wish you could build right here," he said.

"If only," I sighed.

He left with that farmer's nod that means I'm thinking. Months later he reappeared, boots muddy, eyes bright. "I went before the board and the Kilpatrick family," he said. "Asked 'em to partner with ESP and give you the land next door. We'd love nothing more than to honor our fathers in war than to donate the land to the kids of ESP."

It felt like Chutes and Ladders—a roll of grace that lifts you three rows in one move. City-center land costs hundreds of thousands, sometimes millions. We'd been offered "free" land before—always far out, unsafe, or impractical. This was perfect: central, safe, right beside the park where the story began.

Dave and I had almost nothing in common. Young woman, old farmer. Business shoes, work boots. I'd never been to war; his whole family had served. But the biggest things are built by the widest circles—the people who don't look like you, vote like you, or move through life the way you do.

If I'm honest, I don't think Dave grew up around people with disabilities. Early on he kept a friendly distance from our members. But the more he came, the more he edged closer. Bias blinds us to ability. Awareness rewires. I carried my own bias then—born of a few too many patronizing comments aimed at a young woman pitching a struggling nonprofit. Over time, people like Dave rewired me too. Ability kept showing up in unexpected clothes.

The land gift changed everything. We could stay where Martha planted us and still grow. When visitors walked our cracked hallway, we could point through the back door to an overgrown lot and ask them to imagine it full.

One of those visitors arrived courtesy of Big Hearts. A businessman heard our vision at the Georgia Theatre, went home, and told his wife, Kelly, "We're getting involved. We'll host a table in February and fill all eight seats."

Kelly wasn't convinced. She'd never spent time with people with disabilities and could not imagine a "special needs pageant" being anything but awkward. She tried the "I'm not feeling well" escape hatch but showed up anyway—and we surrounded her with strangers.

Big Hearts did what it does. The lights, the music, sequins colliding with belly laughs—joy so unfiltered it disarms you. Kelly watched ability bloom onstage and, I think, inside herself. The next week she walked into my office and said, "I'm only an accountant, but I'm willing to help. Put me to work."

Our problem was visibility. People saw the stage, not our leaky roof. With the VFW land now in view, we needed to let the community see what could be. "ESP is hard to understand, but easy to see," someone once told me. So we built a way to see it.

I called my friend Suzanne. Together with Kelly, we dreamed up weekly women's lunches at ESP—Tuesdays at noon. Tennis teams. Garden clubs. Church circles. Suzanne suggested recruiting coaches' wives. "I'll ask my cousin Lainey to bring them," she said.

The key, we agreed, wasn't just the building. It was the people.

I invited four friends to be our hosts: Amber, Ruthie, Mia, and Hannah. Amber is determined, Mia steadfast, Ruthie creative, Hannah loyal. They share Down syndrome, but otherwise they're wildly different—because if you've met one person with Down syndrome, you've met one person with Down syndrome. Ruthie chose the uniform: pink polos embroidered "Pink Ladies," a nod to *Grease* and a wink to rule-bending friendship.

Each Tuesday, "Laura and the Pink Ladies" greeted guests, offered tours of the leaky roof and the "chocolate sprinkles" in the donated trailers, and served chicken salad with sweet tea. In the middle of my pitch, they'd interrupt with their own stories—hilarious, honest, perfectly timed. Nothing about it felt like the country club. Everything about it felt like us.

It worked. Guests left glowing. Some gave on the spot; others hosted lunches of their own. Coaches' wives invited their circles;

tennis ladies invited other tennis ladies. Kelly kept showing up—her "Why would I go?" quietly transforming into "What can I do?" She found joy in the work the way only someone who's discovered her lane can. She dragged along her friend Betsey, whose husband, Ricky, ran the largest insurance agency in town. One pass through our doors, and Ricky—tough businessman—teared up. He used his influence to open more doors. Years earlier, he'd helped rebuild the Georgia Theatre. Now he wanted to help build a home for ESP.

Ten years later the Pink Ladies still keep their shirts. No matter our age or title, we all ache for an identity that makes a difference.

By summer's end we were at 70 percent of our goal. Close, but not touch it close. I was running out of ideas.

Read the Brags

The message landed on my phone while I propped a bathroom stall door with my foot, waiting out a camper's "business" and dreaming of a future without mildew and window units. "Hi, this is Robyn," a polished Midwestern voice said. "I'd love a tour. We're looking for a few local nonprofits to support."

I took a breath to release my exhaustion and then called her back and borrowed a tone of fresh excitement. "We'd love to have you."

She showed up on one of the steamiest days of summer. Ironed designer shorts, perfect posture. We stepped into our tiny gym just as sunscreen blurred with sweat and counselors tape-wrapped wheelchairs in garbage bags. "What is happening?" she asked, half laughing, half alarmed.

"Mud and Water Wars," I smiled.

Then came the shout that still gives me goosebumps: "FLLLLLLLL AAAAAAAAG!" Morning gathering. Fifty campers ringed the flagpole, college-kid buddies dancing without a trace of self-consciousness. Goon, Trey, and Eric chanted their unit name; Hannah and Amber, faces painted for battle, screamed for theirs. Robyn stood beside me, body stiff at first, then, song by song, she eased in, clapping to words she didn't know. Campers high-fived her as if she'd always belonged.

Between chants I learned her story: corporate trailblazer turned doting grandmother, recently moved from the Midwest to Southern Lake. She and her husband were building their dream home. She told me her builders wanted to host a "dream home" event where patrons could buy tickets to tour her house after completion. "The only way I'll do it," she said, "is for charity." I smiled. I liked her.

Standing there in my thrift-store Chacos and Patagonia shorts, we were different, and yet I couldn't miss how similar we were: we were both building our multimillion-dollar, 14,000-square-foot dream homes. Hers was fully funded; mine was not. . .yet!

Just then the kids began chanting my name, with an adjective in front: "old-lady." Twenty-eight had never felt so ancient. I shuffled to the middle with an imaginary walker and led the favorite camp song, mascara running. Back at Robyn's side, I wiped sweat and said, "We're working to build our dream home too." I told her about replacing the trailers, shade for seizure-prone campers, bathrooms with dignity, a kitchen for popsicles, and cooking demos. The vision sat on my tongue like something I could taste.

Her eyes filled.

Brags followed—our most treasured tradition. It starts with a corny skit and neon cards that read, "I caught _____ doing their best _____. With much love, _____." They sound like trinkets, but you should see the bedrooms wallpapered with them. A diagnosis often arrives with a list of "won't's." Parents begin with papers sharing all the things their children may not accomplish in life, followed by additional papers that are modifications of what their child cannot do educationally. Brags flip the script, naming what is. Naming ability.

A resolution of mine one year was simple: See it. Say it. Science has a name for why it matters—the "production effect." Saying something out loud encodes it deeper. We see it, speak it, hear it, feel it. The more we talk about ability, the more our brains hold on to it. That's how cultures change, one named goodness at a time.

Robyn and I cheered as one camper after the next was celebrated with brags in the middle of the circle. Then, from the middle of the circle a voice boomed, "I caught ROBYN—" and the whole camp roared, "ROOOOOOBYN!" I nudged her forward. "We caught Robyn doing her best to visit ESP for the VERY. FIRST. TIME." The place erupted. "Hip, hip—HOOORAY!"

She stood there stunned. Choked up. Undone.

"I don't think I've ever experienced anything so beautiful," she whispered back in the trailer. We sat shoulder by shoulder at the wobbly table as I slid drawings toward her. Two dream homes. Two different kinds of wonder. At one point, she looked over me and said, "I want to use my dream home to build yours."

And that was that.

We began planning her dream home tours that fall and a fundraising event as a finale. The October tours ended with a harvest-moon party at their home. Robyn and John went all in. She had custom chef coats embroidered for our members; the chef built a menu they could finish at the plate—sprinkling salt, breaking bread, adding the final garnish. He grinned all night, later admitting he hadn't felt that kind of joy in years. A neighbor named David pledged all the drywall for our building. The dad who'd told Robyn about ESP played in the band; his son placed prepared a dish with the chef. Under the October harvest moon we raised $300,000.

That momentum spilled into summer field trips to their club. Our buses rolled up, and kids rolled out in polos and khakis. Neighbors taught tennis and golf, took boat rides, and discovered what happens when ability meets a purpose bigger than itself. All because one woman chose to share her "dream house" with a dream larger than her own.

Change It in One Night

We were $200,000 from the next milestone to break ground. So close.

Where could we gather the same circle again?

I found myself in Barbara Dooley's glass-walled prayer room pondering the question. Barbara—the late Vince Dooley's wife, mother of four, grandmother of a small army, master gardener, hilariously crass, and ferociously kind—was never shy with her voice or her Rolodex. ESP's founder Martha had visited their newborn grandson, Matthew, in the hospital years earlier; ESP meant something to the Dooley family.

"How short are you?" she asked.

"Two hundred thousand," I said.

She didn't blink. "That's not that much in the grand scheme of things. Let's do something about it."

We set a date: twenty couples at the Dooleys' home. We called it "The Night That Could Change It All."

That morning #lovelikeJoseph took the kids to church and told me to go sit on the new property—pray, prepare. I parked by the dilapidated VFW building and crossed the brush to the only tree on the lot. *The Giving Tree* came to mind—the boy who kept asking, the tree who kept giving. As a girl I had felt sorry for the stump. As a mother and a leader I've come to see the story differently: the boy had because the boy asked; the tree was happy because it gave.

Under that tree I asked for $200,000.

I picked up a few leaves and a stick, a promise forming in my hands. If you answer, I'll put something significant right here in this building—an altar of remembrance under a tree.

That evening a light rain fell. It was the Sunday after a Georgia-Auburn game. We arrived with a few ESP friends, and the moment Colin—"Coolman"—saw Barbara, he quoted her famous line, "We'll see ya at Bulldog Kia!" and the house howled. Coolman is as cool as they come: buzz cut, humor ready, and an eye for social media. Coolman has cerebral palsy and is missing an ear and brought the kind of levity no program can produce. Barbara matched him joke for joke. Two people fully themselves, sparking joy the way steel meets stone.

By the end of the night, we had it: $200,000.

I called the architects the next morning about the tree. I wanted a real one planted inside the front room. Their answer was swift. "No freakin' way." Fine. I called the fabricators who make Disney's giant trees. They said yes. Many of our members spend too much of life in clinical rooms and sterile hallways, I wanted them to walk through our doors and see wonder waiting. A tree where brags could be read, songs could be sung, and hope could feel like bark beneath your hand.

Now at 90 percent of the total goal, I called John from the foundation—the one who'd once said, "Call me when you're close." He came to Flag, tears in his eyes, and listened as I shared a small wishlist: a walkway, a new vehicle, and if we were really dreaming, a retaining wall sculpted into an amphitheater—an outdoor stage where our people could be seen and celebrated on ordinary Tuesdays.

Two weeks later his board voted to fund the remaining 10 percent. . .*and* the wish-list walkway, vehicle, and amphitheater of ability.

One night mattered. But it was every small moment before it—the Pink Ladies' polos, Kelly's spreadsheets, Suzanne's invitations, Ricky's phone calls, Robyn's harvest moon, Barbara's gutsy yes, Coolman's jokes, Dave's muddy boots—that changed it all.

See the Ability

The Monday after, I walked into our building and looked at the leaky bucket in the center of the room. Until then it had only read as a problem. Suddenly I could see its ability. It told the truer story—persistence. One drop, then another, then another, until the thing that seemed like a nuisance had quietly kept us afloat. Sometimes the solution is already in the room, doing its job so faithfully we miss its genius.

That's what brags do. They aren't just neon cards; they're a discipline of sight. In a world quick with labels—can't, won't, never—brags are a practiced exchange: inability for ability. See the good. Say it out loud. Make it stick. A parent hears something new about a child. A donor sees something new about a community. A farmer offers land. An accountant starts a movement. A grandmother opens her home. A foundation says yes.

Exchange by exchange, invisible becomes invaluable.

So here is your invitation. Learn who you are and what you bring. Name the strength you keep dismissing because it doesn't look like someone else's. Then spend it. When you catch ability in the wild—on your team, in your child, at the checkout line—say it. You don't need neon paper. A sentence, a note, a text can plant a truth someone carries for a lifetime.

And if you've been staring at your own leaky bucket, tired of the drip, listen closer. You may be holding exactly what a room needs.

One conversation, one shift in perspective, one night. . .can change it all.

CHAPTER **11**

The Jump

What Happens When We Exchange Cowardice for Courage?

> *"Courage is not the absence of fear, but rather the judgment that something else is more important than fear."*
> —Ambrose Hollingworth Redmoon

Bring on the Bucket List

We had shifted our perspective as a community. We'd watched a burned-down theater become a town's rallying cry. We'd seen a dream home turn into a dream for 100 families on a waitlist. Seeds were in the ground. But seeds don't sprout on sentiment alone. They need water. They need motion. They need what Newton would call an outside force.

Our waitlist was moving in a terrible straight line—up and to the right, constant speed, no end in sight. I needed something stronger than good intentions to accelerate the campaign and transfer its momentum to the place where it mattered most: the kids still waiting to belong.

Oddly enough, the answer arrived by way of my own bucket list.

I'd never written it down—who has time for that?—but I knew what sat near the top: jump out of a perfectly good airplane. Like most bucket-list items, money and life had kept that one in the dream category. Graduate school loans and an hourly paycheck will do that to you.

Then a thought landed fully formed: What if a skydiving day could be the outside force? People talk about doing daring things "one day." What if the chance to do it for someone else gave them the push they needed?

I drove my battered red Accord to a rural airfield and met Bill, a veteran pilot with grease on his hands and safety etched into his voice. Could we host a charity skydive? "Sure, kid," he said, eyes twinkling. "I'll give you a deal on the dives. You bring the people. I'll make 'em repeat customers."

Thirty said yes—30 people who had always wanted to jump and finally found their reason. One of them was Annie, an accountant at the university, who arrived in a superhero costume—short spiky hair, bright glasses, and a grin that told me fear would not win the day. Her hand held the hand of her son, Adnan—same hair, same glasses, the kind of smile that lights a hangar and an Elvis-level stage presence that makes a whole room raise its chin. He also has Down syndrome. Annie had always wanted to jump. Loving Adnan, choosing to be his mom, and believing in what ESP does for kids like him gave her the final nudge.

As we suited up, skydiving still sounded fun in theory—exhilarating, even. Standing in line with 29 other jumpers, all I could hear were the headlines in my head. *Nonprofit director dies in charity jump. Pilot error. Parachute malfunction.* Worst of all, my sisters Grace and Kathryn, Kathryn's fiancé Charlie, and #lovelikejoseph were all boarding the same plane. If something happened. . .my poor parents.

I smiled for the photos, grateful on the outside. Inside, fear was doing exactly what fear does—hijacking logic and multiplying with age. Statistics promised I was safe. The numbers didn't calm the amygdala.

Annie and Adnan anchored me. If they could keep stepping toward courage after heart surgeries, schoolyard stares, and a thousand daily micro-battles, surely I could step toward the door of a plane.

At 14,000 feet, tethered to my instructor, we shuffled to the edge. He rocked us back and forth—"One. . .two. . .three. . ."—and we tipped into the roar. For a few impossible seconds we fell through cold, hard, rushing air, and then the canopy thumped open. Silence. Floating. The horizon stretched out like a new map. From 5,000 feet, my troubles were small, and the future looked startlingly clear. I remembered the old Elvis line about the strength to dream and the soul's capacity to fly, and I couldn't help but laugh.

We landed to shouts and tears. Adnan barreled into me with a hug second only to my son's in lifetime rankings. Annie loved it so much she went on to earn her solo certification and has jumped more than 100 times since, helping run The Big Jump every year. Adnan keeps growing his own courage—on ESP stages with his Elvis moves, at Big Hearts, in all the places where lights and love meet.

Touching down, I knew this wouldn't be my last jump. But I also had a hunch I was about to face a scarier leap—with both feet on the ground.

Lead the Rockstar

The Big Jump taught me a personal lesson about fear. An organizational one was waiting around the corner.

My first full-time hire seemed like a unicorn. Kids adored him, parents trusted him, and our college staff followed him. He had a knack for turning everyday moments into stage-worthy scenes. In my mind, we were bandmates—different instruments, same song. I would lead the outward work of raising funds and telling the story; he would take the baton and lead the inside magic with our kids.

We didn't hear the same music.

When I talked about a permanent facility that honored our community and eliminated the waitlist, I pictured more—more space, better pay, additional staff, expanded services. He—and some parents—pictured dilution. Fewer hugs. Less attention. A good thing stretched too thin.

Fear again, wearing a new costume.

I assumed they could see what I saw, that the lunches or evenings I spent with donors, sometimes at their country clubs, were for them as much as for me. I didn't bring them close enough to the "why" to trust the "how." Rumors crept in to fill the space I had left empty. While I was out raising money, the whisper said, I wasn't doing the real work. What they didn't see was me clipping coupons, putting food back on the belt at checkout, and using birthday gift cards for date night.

Scarcity—the shadow that trails so many nonprofits—lowered over us like fog. Under that dim light, fundraising looked like a distraction, even a threat.

By the time I felt the chill, it had seeped into corners I loved. Parents grew distant. My rockstar pulled back. I told myself they were adjusting to my more external role, which was partly true. It was also true that I was afraid to sit down and hear the full weight of their grievances. What if they asked for something I couldn't give? What if the cost of courage was confrontation?

A week before Big Hearts he resigned.

It felt like standing in the open door of the plane with no instructor on my back. The ground was racing toward me—program gaps, event deadlines, a campaign to close, a building about to break ground—and I had no chute packed by someone else. I had to decide whether to step anyway.

For the first time, I thought, I don't know if I can do this.

Gather the People

In the middle of that swirl, a message popped up from Matthew. He was almost 18, one of two boys, grandson of a national-champion coach turned athletic director—Vince Dooley, loved across Georgia for all the right reasons. And Matthew, like his Pop, carried that Dooley spark: mischievous humor, deep determination, eyes that grin before his mouth does. Matthew has cerebral palsy.

"Laura," he wrote, "I want to skydive. My mom will kill me if she knows I messaged you. I want to do it for my eighteenth birthday."

We talked through the risks, the logistics, the thousand ways this could get complicated. Then Matthew made it more complicated in the very best way. He had a dream: three generations—him, his dad, and Pop—leaping for ESP.

I told him it was a lofty dream. I wasn't sure about the legalities. I was less sure an 80-year-old legend would agree.

Matthew had a plan.

"Pop," he said on the phone, "will you skydive for ESP with me and Dad?"

Pop chuckled. "Your dad will never jump. Sure, kid—if your dad jumps, I will."

That evening at dinner Matthew turned to his dad. "Dad, if Pop jumps for ESP, will you jump with us?"

His dad laughed. "Your grandfather's done a lot of things. At his age? He's not jumping out of a perfectly good airplane—even for ESP. So sure. . .if he decides to jump, I will too."

Matthew rubbed his hands together like a cartoon villain. "Call Pop and put him on speaker."

A beat later: "Gentlemen, there will be three generations of Dooleys jumping in April. Get your adult-sized diapers ready!"

Some families inherit businesses. The Dooleys inherited tenacity. Cerebral palsy hadn't tamed it; it had honed it.

Jump day arrived with a field full of cameras and a record-breaking fundraising tally. Most people land from a skydive to a handful of friends and a private high-five. The Big Jump is different. Hundreds gather to cheer the walkers to the plane and the floaters back to Earth. It's a liturgy of courage—a send-off and a welcome home.

I watched as three professionals lifted my 200-pound friend from his chair and suited him up on the hangar floor. Sweat beaded on his forehead as he worked his body to help. Everything in me screamed. . .*This is too much. What are we doing?* But his parents stood beside me, and we all knew: This is what Matthew wanted. This is who he is.

They hoisted him up the two steps into the plane. His dad followed. Then his Pop. My throat tightened.

The minutes in the air felt like hours.

"Jumpers in the sky. Blue skies," the radio finally crackled. We scanned the horizon for dark dots. Nothing. Then—parachutes blooming, one after another, like wildflowers opening all at once. We held our breath.

Matthew's canopy appeared. We could see his legs and hear him yell. Good scream or bad? They slid in and the tandem team held him on the ground for a second. Silence. Then Matthew turned his head, and his smile spilled across the grass.

"That was the first time in my life I felt like I did not have a disability."

His dad and his grandfather landed soon after with matching Dooley grins.

Three stories touched down at once: a father who had faced the slow-motion courage of raising a son with a disability; an 80-year-old coach who had won and lost on giant stages and still said yes to risk; a young man who had just done something his younger self could not have imagined. I thought of all the reasons to say no. If we had, that sentence—the first time—would never have been spoken.

Courage is contagious. Just like momentum, it builds when you spend time near people who keep moving forward despite their obstacles. The more we watch others step into the unknown, the faster our own what-if turns into why not.

Matthew jumped six more times in the years that followed. He moved into his own place with caregiver support and started working. We often don't know how much strength we carry until we stare fear in the face—and step anyway.

I was learning from him. And I was about to need everything he taught me.

Step to the Edge

Spring slid into summer—the busiest season of our year and the brink of our groundbreaking. I had just hired two new directors—hungry, humble, green in all the right ways. I wanted to lead differently this round—closer to the ground, clearer with the "why," more time on the front lines with staff and families. Hire character over charisma. You can train almost any skill. You cannot train a heart.

Their first day landed on the last day of after-school programming, which meant the spring recital. The private school auditorium filled with parents, college interns, board members, and kids ready to show off karate belts, cooking wins, tent-pitching prowess, and Piranha swim medals. We had reviewed the run of show earlier in the week with our program team, all college interns: performances, volunteer recognition, more performances, a look ahead to summer, and finally our big reveal of new program coordinators and their supervisors.

I missed my son's first baseball game to be there. It felt like the right trade.

Toward the end of the night, I stood backstage with the new coordinators—giving pep talks and adjusting collars—when I heard the audio shift. I peeked through the curtain. An unplanned tribute had begun—photos and video set to sentimental music—honoring my former employee. He sat in the audience, arms crossed, smiling while interns spoke. The last one looked out at the families and said she was ashamed our organization would fire someone so special.

Backstage, my pulse hammered in quick bursts. Fired? That wasn't what happened. But a single word, spoken with conviction, can recode a whole story.

I watched the families' faces fall. Shock. Hurt. Confusion. In a breath, I became the villain in a story I'd given my twenties to write.

It was my cue to walk out with a microphone.

The fear was paralyzing. Fourteen thousand feet, edge of the door, but this time the fall would be social, not physical. No harness. No tandem partner.

I looked to my right. Two brand-new leaders met my eyes. They had seen the underbelly of that moment and were still with me. Fear loosened its grip a notch. When you lack courage, borrow it.

I walked to center stage.

"Whoooooo's ready for camp?" I sang out, in the voice our campers know. Their cheers rose—a merciful sound. Parents clapped politely. Skepticism sat like a fog in the rows.

"We all know there would be *no* camp without our directors. I am excited to introduce our two new members of the team." The applause was thin. It didn't matter. I introduced them anyway.

After the recital I hauled boxes and doused trash cans like always and then watched clusters of families wrap my former employee in teary hugs. I felt like a ghost in my own story. Driving home, the ache showed up in all the places I'd sacrificed to be there—the swing I'd missed at baseball, the conversation I hadn't had with staff, the boundary I'd failed to set when I saw the tribute storyboarded by someone else. I told Joseph I was done. I picked up the phone to tell my board chair it was the end for me.

"Sleep on it," she said, voice steady. "You have a choice. You can clean house and start fresh—or you can let the ship go down with the Rockstar captain."

I pictured our ship—the gym with the leaky bucket, the trailers strung like beads behind the building, the new land waiting next door. And I saw faces: The Hulk. Goon. Mia. Caleb. Ruthie, Hannah, Amber. The long list of names still on the waitlist tab.

Fear or something more important?

Just Jump

I didn't sleep much.

In the early light I opened to a story I'd read a dozen times and somehow never needed like this: Nehemiah. A man broken by the need in his city who asked a leader for resources and rebuilt a wall. Halfway through, jealous voices rose. They tried to distract, to lure him away, to smear his motives.

His answer was simple: "I am doing a great work, and I cannot come down." When the rumors multiplied he replied, "There is nothing to these things; you are inventing them in your own mind." And when fear kept nipping at his ankles, he prayed, "Now strengthen my hands."

It felt written for me. Our wall was halfway up. The murmurs were loud. The urge to climb down flared inside me.

Strength, not self-defense. That was the call.

If you want to live a life of big love that results in joy, buckle up: Big love attracts big criticism. Brené Brown says, "If you're going to dare greatly, you're going to get your ass kicked at some point."[1] Not because you've done something wrong, necessarily—because you chose courage. Theodore Roosevelt framed the same truth in his "arena" reminder: It is not the critic who counts. Eleanor Roosevelt added the daily practice: "You gain strength, courage, and confidence by every experience in which you really stop to look fear in the face."[2]

The waiting list had crossed triple digits. Whether anyone questioned my motives or not, the work was working. My motivation was mine to steward. Their experience—their right to hold, grieve, or celebrate.

Would I face the controversy again to fulfill the dream? Every time.

Love has power when it walks on 2 feet and keeps showing up. I loved this organization with everything I had. If that meant stepping back from the role I most enjoyed—camp director—to reorganize, let go of people I cared for, rebuild culture, and lead through misunderstanding, so be it.

Leaders aren't born. They're made in the arena—in daring and failure and the willingness to try again. Leadership is awkward. Courage is agreeing to be awkward on purpose. It looks like owning our misses, apologizing when we've been unclear, asking questions we dread hearing the answers to, drawing lines around gossip, and making decisions that serve the mission even when they don't win the room.

Fear is not the enemy. It's a signal. What you do next writes the story.

I thought of Matthew, strapped to a stranger and smiling at the wide sky. Of Annie, who turned a single jump into a season of courage. Of Adnan's hug. Of Pop saying yes at 80. Of parents whose daily leaps no one applauds—paperwork, meltdowns, meals—and of the kids whose joy keeps teaching us how to live.

So I asked for strong hands and then got to work.

We stabilized the team. We rebuilt communication rhythms. We hired on character, not charisma. We invited parents into the "why," not just the "what," so scarcity had fewer corners to hide in. I kept walking into rooms where I had been misunderstood and choosing to be seen again.

The Big Jump kept doing its holy work outside our walls while the slow work happened inside. Courage—personal and collective—began to spread through us the way a dandelion sends its tiny parachutes into a field of ordinary grass. One seed lands. Then another.

Then another. And one morning you look up and there is yellow where there used to be only green.

Courage isn't the absence of fear. It's weighting the scales honestly and deciding something else matters more—kids who need a place to belong, families who need to breathe, a city that needs to see what's been invisible and call it invaluable. When the moment comes—and it will—step to the edge. Remember who is strapped to you. Borrow courage if you need to. Then jump. See Figure 11.1.

Figure 11.1 The courage continuum

CHAPTER **12**

The Pink Hard Hat

What Happens When We Exchange Invisible for Invaluable?

> "There is a crack, a crack in everything, but it is the light that enters."
>
> —Meister Eckhart

Flush It Out

The heart is brave, but sometimes the body can be a reluctant partner.

Days after the recital—the one where rumors rewrote a story I'd been bleeding to tell—and in the middle of cleansing our culture, training two brand-new directors, and barreling toward the first day of camp and a groundbreaking, my body shut down. I landed in a hospital bed with an abdomen the size of a watermelon and gastrointestinal bleeding the doctors couldn't name. The pain out-sang natural childbirth, and that's saying something. #lovelikeJoseph stood beside me wondering if I would walk back out. I had the same question.

The body keeps score. Mine was running the tally.

From that bed, with ice chips for dinner and morphine doing its best, my mind ping-ponged: The groundbreaking is in days. Camp starts Monday. We're so close. . .my new team. I hired them and then left them. I said I wouldn't. It was a physical cleansing, yes—but I wondered if my mind and heart were getting the cleanse they'd avoided.

If you've ever done a cleanse, there are levels. There's the "reset juice" where you glow and post photos. And there's the colonoscopy cleanse. LORD. HAVE. MERCY. If you know, you know.

Thanks to an ongoing intestinal saga, I now hold a punch card of 10 colonoscopies. On one memorable occasion, I drank the neon orange "juice" right before my son's away football game. Oversight #1: the timing. Oversight #2: the bathrooms were on the home side. Oversight #3: chasing a three-year-old the whole game, cheering for a sixth grader and a husband coaching, and trusting that somewhere our seven-year-old was still alive, bless her heart.

I convinced myself there was time. There is always time...until there is not.

Mid-third quarter, the juice said, "Now." Two choices: humbly inform the coach that his wife had to go home because...*or* channel my inner running back.

I scooped the three-year-old like the actual football and sprinted across the field mid-play.

Not my proudest mom moment.

But if you've done the prep or battled a stomach bug, you understand. Cleansing is messy. The "crap" comes out in all forms and fashions. Lying in the hospital, I realized this season of leadership—pride stripped, truth exposed—was a colonoscopy cleanse. Everything toxic had to come out before anything good could go back in. I hurt and I healed and I read updates from home base.

I missed my children's last day of school.

I missed the rest of staff training.

I missed being strong.

But helplessness does a strange kindness: It tunes your station to other people's pain. A friend bought the teachers' gifts I had promised and delivered them with my love. Another texted, "Checking on you." Small things, invaluable timing. Strapped to a bed, I felt what many of our families feel routinely—another hospital stay, another unknown, the ache of missing life while fighting for it. What breaks your heart fixes your eyes. When I got out, I would do something to make sure no family walked those halls alone.

I thought of Mariah—tan skin, dark hair, dimples, a soundtrack of good music and better style. At eight, a brain tumor snatched the childhood she knew and replaced it with surgeries, treatments, long hospital corridors. Today, she lives life from a wheelchair with limited movement, her days shaped by limitations her younger self couldn't have imagined. The first time she went down an inflatable slide at ESP and the first time she played truly with other kids on a playground were tiny moments that were anything but small.

At first glance, you might say everything was taken. If you ask her family, they'll tell you something rare was given—not the tumor, never the tumor—but what grew in the cracks it left.

Let the Light In

A mentor named the image I couldn't find: kintsugi, meaning "golden joinery." In Japan, when a bowl breaks, it isn't hidden or tossed. It's repaired with lacquer mixed with gold. The cracks don't disappear; they become the art. The piece isn't "like new." But it's more valuable. It's differently whole, its story traced in gold.

Mariah is living kintsugi. The wheelchair doesn't define her any more than gilded seams define the bowl; it's simply part of a story that holds. Her vulnerability, her grit, her capacity for joy—the way she laughs louder now, listens deeper, notices what others rush past—those are the gold veins. Her "before" was whole in one way. Her "now," shaped by struggle, is whole in another—more luminous—way.

Broken isn't the opposite of beauty; it's often the birthplace of it.

We all have cracks—some public, some hidden. Our reflex is to patch, paint, pretend. But what if we honored them, let light find them, and let those very seams become our strength? Compared to Mariah's mountain, my leadership fractures were ant hills. Still, they were making space for gold. Maybe not 24-karat like hers—call mine 10-karat learning—but gold all the same.

Meanwhile, the hospital served Jell-O three times a day like a spiritual discipline. My discharge depended on keeping it down, so I made friends with Frank, who delivered the "decadent delights." Together we started stacking the cups by color—cherry, lime, lemon—into a wobbling Jell-O high-rise. We joked about setting the world record for gelatin architecture.

One afternoon the sun shot through the window, caught the tower, and threw stained-glass light across my wall. It was beautiful. The cracks between the cups made it happen. Ordinary sugar wobbled into beauty because light went hunting for openings.

Maybe that's the point. The breaking lets the light in—and out.

After six days that felt like six months, I could keep down Jell-O. They sent me home just in time for a weekend of rest, the first day of camp, and the groundbreaking. I hobbled into the office Monday, unsteady but determined. My new team wrapped me in worry and welcome. They had led in my absence. Now we would lead together.

We walked out to the field—Georgia sun high, coffee sweating in our hands, 50 campers in plastic hard hats barely containing themselves. Parents raised their phones. Donors mingled with neon-shirted volunteers. Laughter swelled. I climbed—barely—onto a makeshift platform and told the only truths I had: Strength shows up in weakness; our people make our city stronger; hope lives next door in the dirt, and we're about to build a home for it.

Own the Hat

The cracks didn't vanish with one speech. They don't. But I could hold onto the light and start filling them with gold.

The Pink Ladies season had already nudged me toward a truce with pink. (My sisters may or may not have circulated a pre-baby-shower memo for my daughter requesting neutrals; I would neither confirm nor deny.) So when the general contractor handed me a gift at the groundbreaking. . .a pink hard hat. . .I smiled for the photo and bit my tongue.

Because I'm the girl I get the pink hat?

Also, I knew nothing about construction. The hat felt like a label and a hiding place. If expectations were low, maybe I couldn't disappoint.

Weekly construction meetings began anyway. I sat with the foreman, architects, engineers talking of loads and bearings, retention ponds, EPD requirements, trusses. My notebook became a vocabulary list with dollar signs. I was the only woman, the only 20-something, and the only one taking notes. On paper I was leading this project and signing the checks. Around the table, it gave "secretary with a question" energy.

Insignificant. That was the feeling. What did I have to add to a conversation about steel and soil?

Language, I realized, was the gate. If I wanted a seat that mattered, I had to learn to speak construction.

I thought of my friend Greice—a supermodel exterior with a rocket-scientist interior. She moved from Brazil to Georgia for currency trading, spoke zero English, bought a translation pen, spent 100 hours in the Walgreens aisles decoding labels, and taught herself the language. Today she runs a thriving healthcare business and talks about ESP like a proud aunt.

When you don't know the language, you learn it.

So, after bedtime, I opened my laptop and Googled every term I didn't know from that week's meeting. I called construction-savvy board members between naps and school pickups. Little by little, the blur began to sharpen. I learned enough to ask the right questions—about timelines, change orders, budget creep. I didn't become an engineer. I became the person who knew our people, our programs, and how the building needed to work for them.

Becoming rarely waits for permission. You put on the hat—pink, if necessary—and do the work. Somewhere in the mess you become exactly what your organization, your family, your dream needs.

Eventually, I made peace with the pink. In fact, it turned out useful. As the signer of checks and the decider of "yes/no/maybe, but cheaper," the foreman needed to know when I hit the site. For the crew members who didn't speak English, the pink was unmistakable. Word traveled fast: The pink (and heels) had arrived.

Somewhere between my first "What's a truss?" and our final punch list, the hat that once made me feel small became a badge. A symbol that used to whisper insignificant had become invaluable.

Rock the Rock

Progress at first was geologic—slow and steady, which is code for excruciating when the waitlist is staring at you like a clock you can't silence. Big Hearts loomed, and donors would want a dazzling update.

We had one. We'd hit rock.

If you've built anything bigger than a birdhouse, you know rock is the plot twist no one wants. You can't grade properly until you break it up and haul it out. Translation: more time, more money, more mud.

Day after day we stared at a sloshing pit while Georgia winter rain snickered. It felt like someone strapped ankle weights on the last lap.

Two weeks before Big Hearts my son handed me a crumpled Sunday school paper. "A wise man builds his house on the rock, Mom."

It might as well have been a billboard.

Of course we hit rock.

We talk about "rock bottom" like it's a curse. Ask someone on the other side—often it's the foundation of the rebuild. Rock is solid. Our building would hold heavy electric wheelchairs, dance parties that shook the rafters, storms that rattled windows. Under it all, we would want rock.

The geotech report finally told us how much we were dealing with and what kind. The solution arrived in five blue-jeaned workers, a drill rig, and a small supply of dynamite. They gave us the date. I rallied our staff with hard hats and popcorn. If we were paying for delay, we might as well get a show.

We lined the temporary fence like kids at a county fair. The foreman glanced over as if to say, "Bless your hearts." The countdown began.

Ten. . .nine. . .eight. . .we held our breath. . .three. . .two. . .one. . .

Poof.

A polite puff of dirt. No fireworks. The ground politely considered wobbling and decided against it.

My staff looked at me like this was the field trip? I grinned. Then laughed. Then we all laughed. I cranked "Ain't No Mountain High Enough" on my phone. Jake—our nearly seven-foot program director—shimmied. Kalon skipped circles. Ashley and Katarina twirled. Even Gina, our bookkeeper and ESP mom, smiled like someone had just balanced the budget.

Anticlimactic or not, we were closer. And we were doing it together. That counted.

Part of my new leadership rhythm with a growing team was this: We celebrate every inch. Windows arrive? Donuts. Permit issued? Pop the confetti cannons we found in a closet. A slab poured between storms? Group selfie in the mud. Teach your team to savor small steps, and one morning they wake up with a building.

At Big Hearts we told the not-so-epic explosion story and showed photos of footings and slab curing under gray skies. Standing backstage, I saw the rock differently—less like a delay, more like a gift. Our firmest footing had come from the obstacle I wanted most to avoid. And the boulders we broke up that day sit in the landscaping as a reminder.

Dar las Gracias a las Manos

The superintendent from our construction company was a tall, snaggle-toothed New Yorker with a heart that tried hard to hide behind a foul mouth. We developed a rhythm. I pitched a ridiculous idea; he rolled his eyes and found a way to make it happen. He let me learn to drive a tractor but would light up a subcontractor for leaving cigarette butts on site. He snuck donors and members past the gate for progress tours and then barked at guys for tracking mud inside. My kind of paradox.

I called him "Number Seven" because we had six full-time staff and, whether he liked it or not, he'd become the seventh. First to arrive, last to leave, commuting an hour-and-a-half each way. Something about this project had hooked him. Maybe one day I'd hear the whole story.

One afternoon Seven grabbed me when a new curb-and-gutter crew arrived. I pulled on my Georgia-red-clay gardening boots (it's a vibe), popped on the pink hat, and followed him through the "Do Not Enter" gate.

He stopped the crew. The men eyed him, then me, annoyed. Time is money, and I was interrupting both. Seven muttered in Spanish and gave me the floor.

On the other side of the fence, after-school program was buzzing. A teen navigated a wheelchair obstacle course while friends with Down syndrome cheered like it was the Olympics.

I opened my mouth and produced the only Spanish that surfaced: "El baño. . .y. . .¿puedo tener una margarita?" Nailed it.

The crew chuckled. Seven grinned his snaggletooth grin. It was time to pivot. I pointed to the men and then to the field. "What you are doing is creating a special place for them."

Seven translated, but honestly, I think they got it before the words caught up.

I pointed again to their hands. "Sus manos. . ." Then to our friends, ". . .están construyendo un lugar para todos." Your hands are building a place for everyone.

Silence slid over the site. Sunglasses came off. Calloused knuckles wiped quick tears.

"Gracias," I said, because it was the truest thing.

They nodded, murmured to Seven, and went back to work faster than before.

That evening the company president left me a voicemail. My stomach dropped. I pictured an HR seminar on "What Not to Say in Spanglish."

"Laura," he said when we connected, "I don't know what you told my guys today, but they came to me as a group and said they didn't want a paycheck for your project. These are men who work every day to feed their families."

He paid them anyway—and refused to charge us for the curb and gutter.

No PowerPoint. No pitch deck. No case statement.
They saw it. They felt it. The exchange.

We all want to be part of something bigger than ourselves. Many of those men build beauty that becomes invisible the day the ribbon is cut. Here, they met the people who would roll those curbs and wheel over those gutters. Their hands went from insignificant to invaluable in a single afternoon.

Joy translates. Across language, age, income. When we're seen as valuable—and get to give value—everything shifts.

Let It Radiate

The curb and gutter was one story among a thousand. If you remember *Extreme Home Makeover*, imagine that energy stretched over years—a community rallying in waves.

The more people saw the need and felt they had something to give, the more they brought others along. Reciprocity started rippling.

Jon, a board member, donated engineering and became my construction translator and co-project manager. He grew up the son of a butcher who quietly supported Special Olympics. What we model in front of our kids is often the character they wear as adults.

Jon introduced me to John (with an "h"), an influential paving contractor. John offered to donate all the paving in-kind and pulled his friend Dan into the mix—saving tens of thousands. It was contagious—the giving and the invitations.

We timed tours for golden afternoons when programs spilled joy across the field. People came braced for a pitch and left giving before we asked.

Tony and Denise, dear family friends who run Kitchen Designs, came to measure for counters and cabinets. We sat with members during snack time, and when they asked what kind of counters we wanted, I said, "Laminate will be just fine." They smiled and donated 100 percent of the cabinets and countertops for the activity rooms and kitchen— hello, granite—because details tell people what you think they're worth.

Our banker Lorie sent her husband to measure for office cabinetry; he donated those, too.

Dalton Carpet One donated carpet and flooring and even helped imagine a tile wall that makes our kitchen sing.

A chamber friend introduced us to The Sign Bros; they donated all the building signage.

A dad from my kids' school donated every shingle.

One of Jon and John's partners gifted significant landscaping.

A local company known for transforming barnwood built a feature wall and a conference table so heavy it had to be assembled in the room. Later I learned the owner's wife had a sister who passed away from multiple disabilities. This was their way to honor her.

Every time a new set of hands touched the project, something was exchanged. With each exchange, traction grew. And as traction grew, the waitlist began to feel less like a mountain and more like a series of switchbacks. Climbable.

Companies told me their teams were different after being on-site. Purpose had snuck into staff meetings and Monday mornings.

Sociologists might call it "social capital." Marcel Mauss simply called it The Gift: reciprocity as the glue of communities—the mutual giving and receiving that makes belonging possible. When giving originates inside a culture instead of as a tax write-off or box to check, it radiates. The material gift produces an emotional return that is so satisfying you can't help but keep giving—and invite others to join. Deloitte found that nearly 9 out of 10 Americans think companies that sponsor volunteer activities create better workplaces. Cone/Porter noted that almost 80 percent of people feel a deep personal connection to companies with a strong purpose. Harvard linked corporate social performance to financial performance. CECP reported that companies with robust community investment see stronger economic outcomes and morale. Translation: Radiant reciprocity is good for the bottom line and the human soul.

I watched it play out in red clay and sawdust. Joy moved through crews and board rooms and break rooms, and no one wanted to be the last link in the chain.

Press the Hands

Inside, wires threaded through walls like veins and HVAC ducts snaked across ceilings. Outside, the property still read Georgia clay.

In one meeting we mapped the paving schedule, and an image I couldn't shake became a sentence that wouldn't leave:

"When we pour the front walk, could our members press their hands in the concrete?"

Silence. Then a stack of reasons why not: OSHA. Heavy equipment. Gravel ruts. Fencing. Wheelchairs and walkers don't tango with construction zones. Could we do blocks off-site and install them later? Bricks we could set at the end?

It all felt. . . safe. And wrong.

Our construction manager, Adam, finally leaned in. "We find a way for everyone else to get on the property and play their part. There has to be a way. How many kids is this? A few?"

I smiled. Adam got it. "Yeah, just a few. About a hundred."

He didn't flinch.

The following Sunday, Adam made it happen. The crew laid temporary boards like a pilgrim path through the site and opened the gate. We passed out hard hats that slid over small ears and onto big smiles. A cement mixer hummed to life and started pouring the walk that would welcome thousands for years to come.

One by one, we took hands—some curled tight, some flapping with joy, some steady, some shaking—and we rolled, carried, and walked our friends down the path to the front curb. We knelt. We lifted. Parents cried. Staff cried. I cried. We pressed hands into wet gray and traced initials in the center of each print.

"What the hand does, the mind remembers," Maria Montessori said. We wanted their bodies to remember this: This is your place. Your hands helped make it. Your presence is not an afterthought; it is the point.

A cool spring sun warmed our backs. As we straightened and bent again, imprint after imprint, I felt light seep into places that had been dark: the hospital room, the rumor-riddled recital, the rock and the mud and the not-so-epic explosion. Light doesn't just pierce. It pools in the cracks and makes mosaics of them.

In every stage of the build—pink hat, stubborn rock, a curb poured by men who rarely hear thank you, fingerprints pressed into concrete—what looked insignificant revealed itself invaluable.

That is the nature of radiant reciprocity: give what you have, invite others to do the same, and value multiplies in ways you couldn't have planned. Our friends with disabilities were never just recipients; they were the most invaluable gift to everyone who came to build. Their joy, their being, their hands—those didn't just mark concrete. They imprinted people.

It's easy to overlook what doesn't glitter. But if we press the "hands" we've been given—our skills, our relationships, our presence—into the work before us, the light will find the cracks and radiate far beyond our reach.

Somewhere in your life there's a pink hard hat—something you're tempted to dismiss, a symbol that makes you feel small. There's a rock slowing you down, a curb poured by unseen hands, a walkway waiting for fingerprints. Lean into them. Invite them in. Honor the cracks. Because what looks small today may be the most invaluable gift tomorrow—and the very place where the light gets in (see Figure 12.1).

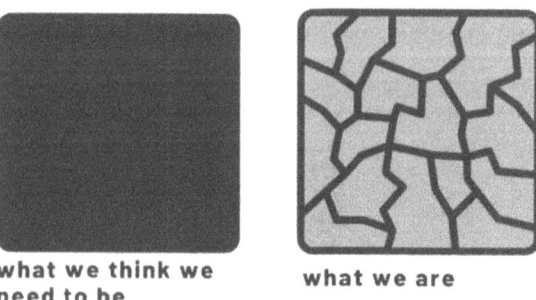

Figure 12.1: The myth of wholeness

SECTION THREE

From Them to Us

When we shift our perspective and cultivate the art of truly seeing, we transform what we value. And what we value reshapes the patterns we live by and the rhythms that guide us.

From my window, I watch yellow daffodils emerge each spring. Some years, they arrive early—bold and hopeful—only to wither when winter reminds them it isn't finished. This year, the daffodils are especially lovely, luscious, and bright. Just before them lies a patch of moss, a quiet byproduct of sporadic lawn care since our family moved in. And nestled in that moss are dandelions.

These dandelions—which I proudly allow to grow—are the first to rise, standing firm through shifting weather. They feed the bees, pollinate other blooms, and pave the way for what follows. I often wonder: if a dandelion could speak, what would it say of the daffodil? Would it boast, "We arrived first. It's because of us the daffodils stand a chance."

Or would the quiet wisdom of nature never entertain such a thought?

In *The Art of Loving*, Erich Fromm names both the gift and the ache of being human: "Man is gifted with reason; he is life being aware of itself."[1] This awareness, Fromm then argues, creates man as a separate entity—and it is this separation that is "the source of all anxiety."

We, in our reasoning, divide ourselves: them, those people, not me, they. And yet, nature—in its seamless harmony—keeps offering us a different way.

The dandelions outside my window are not in isolation. They are part of a living, breathing whole. Each contributes what it has, unburdened by comparison. The dandelion gives its goodness and then multiplies it—its final act an offering to the future.

The biggest thing that prevents us from joy is individualism.

The interconnectedness of nature is calling to us. The synchronicity of sun and rain, of roots and wings, of flowers and soil—all working in quiet, fierce collaboration. There is no hierarchy in this system. No "us versus them." There is only *us*.

And when *us* becomes the goal, everything multiplies. When *us* is found, joy abounds.

THE ART OF "US"

CHAPTER **13**

The Welcome

What Happens When We Exchange Hesitation for Hospitality?

> "I've learned that people will forget what you said, people will forget what you did, but people will never forget how you made them feel."
>
> —Maya Angelou

Shake the Pom-Pom

It's one thing to be invited. It's another thing to feel wanted when you arrive.

Five days before opening day—and six before the first day of camp—time thinned to the finish line. The Georgia heat pressed its palm against our backs as the punch list grew faster than we could cross things off. From morning till dark, we hustled: hanging letters that would spell welcome in a dozen small ways, arranging couches so parents could exhale, sorting supplies into labeled bins, and arguing with packing tape that refused to cooperate.

Carter, our tall board member, flew in from Texas and brought his whole family. They spent hours wrangling IKEA furniture in the activity room, their knuckles baptized by Allen wrenches. We all still flinch a little when we see one of those tiny silver tools; they're like flashbacks in metallic form.

Plenty could have waited. The framed photos didn't have to be up. The art supplies could have stayed boxed. We could have set a skeleton stage and filled in the rest later. But we weren't just opening a building; we were writing a prologue. The stories of our families kept echoing—years of showing up to places not built with them in mind. I couldn't shake one mom's story. It wasn't rare; maybe that's why it haunted me.

It was her first time trying a city recreation program with her daughter who has cerebral palsy. On the drive over her stomach twisted: *Will they help us? Is there a place to change her? Will someone meet us at the door?* When they arrived, every accessible parking space was taken, by people without handicapped stickers on their cars. She parked where she could and then muscled through 20 hot minutes unloading equipment, sweat beading at her collarbone. "This is going to be amazing," she told her girl, as much for herself as for her daughter.

There was no automatic door. No one hovering to say, "We were waiting for you." She wedged the heavy door with her foot, swung the chair with her hips, and let it slam into her back. Inside, fluorescent lights hummed, sound bounced, a volunteer stared too long, a staffer peered up from nametags and then back down again.

"Hi, we're new. Where should we go?" she asked.

A cleared throat. A pointed finger toward an office. In 30 minutes, the message was clear: This place isn't ready for you. Like too many places before it, the room whispered, *You don't belong here.*

When I think of belonging, I don't think of big banners or perfect signage. I think of Nana's house. Seven hours in the car, windows down, hair sticky with summer, and then sprinting up those steps. Nana and Pawpaw would startle to standing, their bodies slower than their faces—eyes bright, hands already reaching. Dinner waited warm on the counter: corn, peas, okra, ham, rolls you could tear with your fingers. Banana splits at the ready, toppings lined like jewels. Chairs pulled out, blankets folded, the house prepared. . .not for "guests" but for "us."

That is welcome: a place that says, *We thought of you long before you got here.*

Most people haven't felt that outside their family's living room.

As opening day crept close, that mom's story sat on my shoulder. All the unwelcoming rooms she'd wheeled through, the stares, the barriers, the exhaustion that settles into your bones when every door is a test. What if, here and now, we could be the place that shouted welcome?

Our old space had done its best. We had squeezed hospitality into a loud gym and under a leaky roof, but no greeting can fully outrun a building that tells a different story. This building was our chance to make the room say what our hearts had been saying for years.

So we went all in.

Everything mattered: balloons clustered like small suns, a cake in the gym, pom-poms in buckets, name-tagged shirts in every size. Board members who thought they'd be pouring ice water found themselves shoveling mulch in sundresses and dress shoes. Tractors wrapped up grading while fresh asphalt radiated heat like a stovetop. Makeup surrendered. Sweat did what sweat does. Smiles stayed anyway.

At 4 p.m. they would arrive. This time would be different.

I pinballed through the building: balloons, check. Cake, check. Paper towel rolls, loaded. Paint drips, scrubbed. Floor stickers, aligned. Anticipation thumped like a drumline. This wasn't about showing off new square footage. It was about the people we loved walking into a place that loved them back. It was about saying, *We see you*—and today the building would say it with us.

A building is just a building until people walk in. Then it becomes a promise kept.

Gather at the Threshold

By 3 p.m. the parking lot was a sea of shade-seekers. We passed out water, pointed folks toward the tented pockets of breeze, and—for this one time—held everyone outside. We wanted members to be the first through the doors; it was their homecoming. Families, neighbors, business owners, the Chamber—700 people stood in the heat because hope makes the searing air feel like little more than urgency.

Our team laced fingers and stepped forward together. I called our ESP members to the front and lifted the mic:

> "Three hundred and sixty-four days ago, we broke ground right here. But this journey began 30 years ago with our founder, Martha Wyllie. Three years ago, a small seed was planted—a hope for a home designed with each of you in mind. And over time, this community watered that seed: the VFW, the Mayor and Council, our board, donors, and dream builders. Thank you for believing in a place that proclaims with every beam and brick: *Everyone belongs*. From a small seed, a mighty trunk has grown.
>
> "But what is a tree for if not shade? To our ESP families: This is your tree, your shade, your home. May it be a place of laughter, joy, and unconditional welcome. Welcome home, ESP."

We cut the ribbon together: my hand, a hand with Down syndrome, the curved fingers of cerebral palsy, the rocking arms of autism—all of us at the hinge point. The ribbon snapped, and something in me did too. It wasn't just an opening; it was a tearing through years of "not yet" into a chorus of "yes."

People poured in—eyes wide, tears ready. They filed past the swap shop, past the parent lounge, and past the tree at the entrance, the one I'd once stood beneath on an empty lot and prayed under like it was a cathedral.

We floated from room to room, receiving hugs and damp cheeks, giving the same back. Between one embrace and the next I started looking for Number Seven. I wanted to put him in the path of the people his crew had built for. He wasn't on the walkie. Not in the gym. Not in the art room. I finally found him in the sensory room, shoulders hunched, a big man small and red-faced.

"What's going on?" I asked.

He swallowed. "This day. . .it's a lot." He paused and then let the rest out like a flood. "I should've told you. My brother had special needs. When I was a kid, he hurt me once. My parents sent him away. I've carried the guilt ever since—for not knowing him and for being the reason he wasn't with us. He's gone now. Building this. . .if my family had had a place where we weren't stared at but welcomed—" His voice cracked. "It would've been different."

This man who barked orders and kept a job site in line stood in a room designed for calm, and the boy inside him finally found some. We stood there quietly, and I let him hug me like he was five. The project had given him a gift I couldn't have planned: a small redemption, a place to set down a bit of what he'd carried.

The building had more stories to write that day—each one a reminder that hospitality is not just for guests. It's for all of us, because welcome draws out what's beautiful and lets it breathe.

Close the Gap

The ribbon had snapped, but the real unveiling was happening in faces: people reading themselves in the walls, the rooms, the way the light fell.

A dad stopped me in the lobby, hands on my arms, words catching. "People don't build beautiful things for people with disabilities," he said finally. "My daughter's classroom is a trailer behind the school. We always get the leftovers. I thought this would be bigger. But I didn't know it would also be this beautiful."

He was right. For months I had obsessed over function—automatic doors, wide hallways, family bathrooms, sensory spaces. But standing in that room, I felt the deeper truth: beauty is not a luxury; it is dignity made visible. When the world keeps handing you leftovers, the subtext is constant: You're less. But when a room is prepared for you with care—when every detail whispers you matter—something inside stands taller. Beauty begets beauty; it calls goodness forward.

I looked him in the eyes. "We do build beautiful things—because you are."

Years earlier a generous board member sent my husband and me to the Ritz-Carlton for an anniversary night. Our dusty Honda Pilot looked like it had snuck into prom as we handed over the keys. "You can park her next to the Maserati," Joseph told the valet with a grin. Inside we were greeted by name and handed cool towels, fruit-infused water, and linen that felt like a poem. At first I felt like an imposter. But honest hospitality has a way of unshrinking you. By checkout, I wasn't different but something was: I carried the sense that maybe I was worth that level of care. Maybe I belonged in spaces that noticed.

What if our families left here feeling that? Not just served—but cherished.

Father Greg Boyle has spent decades building kinship with people who have been told by the world, *You are not welcome.* He says the measure of our compassion isn't in serving those on the margins but in recognizing we are them and they are us. The word he uses often is delight—delighting in the person in front of you without first weighing their worthiness. Not a reward. A recognition.

Delight is a posture. And kinship begins when we move closer.

That's easy to say. It's harder when discomfort shows up first. We don't talk about it much because the word is strong, but here it is: sometimes disgust gets to the door before delight can. Pixar put "Disgust" on the *Inside Out* dashboard for a reason. It's a primal reflex—originally helpful for survival—that misfires in social spaces.

If we're honest, we've all felt it, even for a blink: the flinch at drool, the recoil from a smell, the urge to step back when a behavior confuses us. Jerry Seinfeld once joked that we'll kiss someone on the head and then scream if one of their hairs shows up in our egg salad. Same hair. New context. Suddenly vile.

Could the same be true with people? Out of context—out of the rooms where we've learned to see—human differences can trigger a reflex that keeps us apart.

At ESP, I've watched that reflex get rewired. A 19-year-old volunteer is paired with a camper who has cerebral palsy—who drools, whose nose needs wiping, who needs help in the bathroom. On day 1, you can see the hesitation. By day 5, that same volunteer is wiping a mouth with one hand, sipping a Coke with the other, laughing about the lunch menu, and planning what to wear for talent night. Disgust dissolved. Delight arrived.

What changed? Not the camper. Proximity. Time. A choice to stay. Delight blooms when you're close enough to see the person, not just the label.

This isn't only about camp. It's about neighborhoods, churches, workplaces—anywhere people share space. We can train our bodies to move toward instead of away.

Unreasonable, on Purpose

Will Guidara took over one of the most lauded dining rooms in the world and realized excellence wasn't enough. He wrote "unreasonable hospitality" on a napkin and then went about embodying it. Years later, Eleven Madison Park was named #1 in the world—not only because of food but because of care. He argues hospitality shouldn't be quarantined to five-star hotels; it should be the operating system of any organization where humans gather.

Why? Because hospitality accrues what Will calls emotional equity—the trust and warmth that build one small act at a time. Emotional equity is good for morale and mission. It creates spaces people want to be—and come back to. It reminds them they are worthy of being there.

We felt that at ESP as we opened those doors. Hospitality wasn't a department. It was the water we wanted to swim in.

Practice the Welcome

At ESP, hospitality is one of our hallmarks. We talk about it, hire for it, budget for it, practice it. Our guiding value—joyful hospitality—calls us to bake intentional delight into everything we do.

It shapes how we welcome new families: a parking space saved, a greeter at the door, paperwork we fill out with them instead of handing over a clipboard. It changes how we honor volunteers: thank-you notes that mention something only they did, a shout-out at flag for the person who quietly stayed late to clean. It reframes how we thank donors: not just a receipt, but a story with a name and a face, and an invitation to see the room their gift prepared. It colors how we treat each other when we're tired and behind and the copier is jamming again.

What waits on the far side of hospitality?

- **For businesses:** Belonging—the single strongest driver of engagement. People stay where they feel wanted, not merely tolerated.
- **For families:** Homes our grown children want to return to, because the chairs are pulled out and they know they can exhale there.
- **For friend groups:** Regular tables with extra chairs; calendars that bend to make room; a text that says "come as you are."
- **For churches:** Foyers that feel like living rooms and sanctuaries that sound like kinship, where people experience Jesus because they were seen before they were corrected.
- **For all of us:** A recovery mission—to remember we were never meant to do life alone.

Individualism is a stingy storyteller; it starves joy. Hospitality multiplies joy by multiplying we. Maybe that's why welcome starts with we.

I felt that "we" the first week I walked into ESP and met Ruthie, Hannah, and Mia. They lit up when they saw me—on day one, and again on day two, and again on day three—before I had offered them a single thing. They didn't require my résumé. They didn't demand I prove my usefulness. They delighted first. It changed me.

Maya Angelou was right: People forget speeches and spreadsheets. They remember the feeling in the room that day. I felt wanted. That changed what I wanted to build.

So as we opened that beautiful building—trusses high, mulch laid, cake sliced, gifts bagged—I kept listening for the room to say what we believed. In every corner the building whispered, *You belong.*

Work the Beauty

All afternoon we watched people try the rooms on like a new coat. In the art studio, a mom ran her fingers along the counter and then, without meaning to, along her own arm—as if to check that she was in fact here. In the kitchen, a dad opened a cabinet, shut it, opened it again, and smiled at the smoothness of a hinge someone had donated. In the amphitheater, siblings sat on the warm concrete and leaned into each other's shoulders while a teen in noise-canceling headphones swayed to music only he could hear.

Hospitality lives in menus and doorways and floorplans, yes. But it also lives in the parts you can't photograph: the way the front desk welcomes a meltdown instead of shrinking from it; the way a staffer learns a sibling's name; the way we don't make people earn their way to belonging.

Dr. Boyle says joy comes from kinship—and kinship begins with delight.[1] We train for that. We tell our college staff that their first job is not to manage a behavior but to love a person. We remind ourselves that the goal is not compliance but connection, and connection grows fastest in the soil of delight.

It sounds soft until you see what it does to fear. It disarms it.

Remember My Brother

Late in the day I found Seven again, this time outside under the tree. The crowd had thinned. He was quiet, a man who had run out of words. We stood there a while, watching families move through a building that had once existed only as lines on a page.

"You gave my brother a place," he said finally.

"I think your brother gave us one," I said.

He nodded. Sometimes hospitality is as simple as letting a sentence land and not trying to make it tidy.

Feel the Culture

A few weeks after opening, I stood near the front door and watched a scene I can't shake. A first-time mom paused at the entrance. Her daughter's wheelchair made a soft squeak; her hands trembled on the push handles. The automatic button was ready for her but not needed. One of our greeters stepped toward her with a grin like sunrise.

"We've been waiting for you," she said.

We had.

The mom exhaled a sound that was more than breath. In 30 seconds, hospitality had moved mountains we couldn't see.

Here's the thing about a culture of welcome: It's not magic. It's a thousand small decisions practiced on purpose. It's choosing delight over distance, again and again, until the building hums with it. It's letting beauty do what it does best—call out the beauty in people.

Underline the We

Welcome, at ESP, is not a program we run once a quarter. It is who we are trying to become every day. Joyful hospitality is our posture. We fail at it sometimes. We begin again.

It shapes our first emails and our last goodbyes. It steers staff meetings, interrupts to-do lists, reroutes busy people toward slower conversations. It reminds us to leave margin in our schedules, because the best moments of hospitality are rarely on the calendar.

And it asks something of all of us: to decide that the person in front of us—whoever they are, however they arrive—is worth delighting in, not because of what they give us but because of who they are.

What waits on the other side of hesitation?

- Rooms that feel like living rooms
- Teams that trust each other
- Families who come back because they stopped bracing
- Communities that start to look each other in the eye again

Most of all, joy. Because joy loves company.

I learned my first "we" at ESP from Ruthie, Hannah, and Mia. They didn't check my name tag. They didn't audition me. They just let their faces tell me what their hearts already knew: *You can sit with us.*

That's the movement I want to be part of—the one where doors don't merely open; they call your name. Where hospitality isn't a tactic; it's a way of seeing. Where we stop handing people leftovers and start setting out the best we have. Where the first words are "We've been waiting for you" and the last are "Come back soon."

As we flung those doors wide that first night—sweat-slick, mascara-smudged, Allen-wrench bruised—I realized this was more than a grand opening. It was a declaration. A promise that the most important thing we would ever build wasn't a roof or a room or a ribbon to cut. It was a culture.

Joy lives on the far side of hesitation. It meets us when we lean in, when we choose to move closer, when we practice delight until it becomes reflex. The rooms we fill with that kind of welcome ripple far beyond our walls—into schools and offices, ball fields, and grocery lines—until strangers start feeling like neighbors again.

So here's your invitation: Step toward someone you've been stepping around. Save them a seat. Learn their name. Pull the door, hold it, and say the line every heart is aching to hear.

We've been waiting for you!

CHAPTER 14

The Blend

What Happens When We Exchange a Problem for a Purpose?

> *"Your purpose is not the thing you do. It's the thing that happens in others when you do what you do."*
> —Jelani Memory

Let the Beans Bounce

Hospitality is contagious. I didn't know that opening a building could infect an entire community with a desire to welcome—but it did. Think of a dandelion: One parachute seed takes off, lands in an unlikely place, and takes root. Real movements rarely begin with grand gestures; they start with small seeds carried by ordinary wind.

The summer we opened our dream building, everything changed. For the first time, our doors could swing wide enough to welcome not only campers, families, and college staff but also the people who lived outside our disability community—especially our business partners. Our old space had forced us to keep things tight; our new home let us invite the town in.

We started hosting "corporate partner days." Teams arrived with boxed lunches and ball caps, learning names and helping with activities and then lingering because something in the room felt different—lighter, kinder, more human. CEOs and HR leaders pulled me aside and said it out loud: "This is the right thing to do. . .but it's helping us, too. Our people go back more joyful, more loyal, even more productive. Honestly? It helps the bottom line."

I kept hearing it. It helps us. And I started to wonder: What about the companies that can't come? The employees on a line or in a far-off office? Joy like this shouldn't be contained by four walls.

For the first time in my career, I also felt. . .comfortable. We'd moved in. We had eliminated the waitlist. We finally had enough. Did I really want to disrupt that?

One afternoon I stood in our commercial teaching kitchen, stainless steel shining like a promise. Beside me: Jake, my program director, part little brother and part co-conspirator, all heart, the kind of person who could turn a wild idea into a run of show.

"Jake," I finally said, "what about the businesses we can't get here? What if we could take ESP to them?"

Our anthem had always been to serve people with disabilities. But the truth that had come for me, over and over, was that the people I thought I was serving were serving me—and everyone who met them—right back. I'd watched it in others, too: a few minutes in our space, and something rewired. Could that happen in other rooms?

Years earlier, we'd run a seasonal coffee stand called Bouncing Beans, staffed by our adults. It wasn't fancy—Folgers-level coffee for sleepy counselors—but the purpose was deeper: meaningful work. Eighty-seven percent of adults with disabilities who want to work can't find a job. Bouncing Beans was our first small push against that number.

Jake started pacing—always a sign something good was brewing. "What if we combine it all?" he said. "Real jobs for our adults. Real engagement for companies. And we take it to them."

I could see it: a traveling coffee cart, staffed by our people, rolling into offices and shop floors with the same joy that filled our building. "They have a joy everyone needs," I said. "How about. . .Java Joy?"

We both promised to sleep on it. Neither of us did. By midnight we'd texted a name, a logo, a short story, and a wild plan. A Kickstarter later, we had $15,000—enough for a simple cart, supplies, a website, and our first hires.

Sometimes the biggest problems hide the clearest purpose.

Just Keep Moving

We sat in the conference room batting around details. Someone asked, "We can't just call them baristas, can we?"

"No," another said, "too ordinary."

"Joyristas?" I offered. "Barista plus joy."

We tried it out loud. It stuck. A title that named the real product we wanted to deliver.

Now we needed a first gig. I texted Lorie.

Lorie is a banker who knows everyone and somehow makes each person feel like the only one in the room. At 30 she had survived a massive brain tumor while raising two daughters. Nothing about her compassion is theoretical. When we told her the idea, she didn't blink. "I have a Santa coffee for the Chamber at the bank in two weeks," she said. "Can you be ready?"

Lorie is a master of "yes" when "yes" serves a purpose. She reminds me that purpose and profession are not the same thing. Your job title is what you do; your purpose is what happens in others when you do it. Lorie sells loans and builds communities at the same time.

We built the cart, trained the Joyristas, ordered shirts, and practiced pouring. Jake tackled brewing and uniforms; I took bookings and social. We had a story, a logo, a janitor cart—and a date on the calendar.

One big decision remained: the coffee.

Choose the Flavor

If you've ever shown up to a bake sale and bought a stale cookie anyway, you know how compassion can outpace quality. But if Java Joy would stand on its own—not as pity coffee but as great coffee—we needed excellence. Those Burger King crowns from our early days haunted me; good intentions aren't enough.

Enter Jittery Joe's, the Athens institution with the orange cups. Michael, their CEO, was a tech-guy-turned-coffee-guy with a soft spot for ideas that start in service. When Jake pitched him, he said, "If we do this, we'll do it right. Let's bring in the experts."

He set up a blind cupping at the roastery: four orange cups labeled only with numbers. Inside: Ethiopian, Ecuadorian, Guatemalan, and one "mystery." The room smelled like caramel and citrus and possibility. We handed each taster a single coffee bean to vote with and told them to drop it in their favorite cup.

We watched our Joyristas most closely. When the voting ended, every bean from them had landed in cup four.

Michael grinned. Cup one—Ethiopian. Cup two—Ecuadorian. Cup three—Guatemalan.

Cup four? The mystery.

A blend of all three.

Of course it was. A blend. Diverse notes. Different strengths. Together, balanced and better—exactly the story we wanted to tell.

Blends outsell single-origin coffees for a reason; our palates are wired to enjoy balance. Communities are, too. But blends don't happen by accident. They're crafted on purpose.

We inked a partnership. Our lawyer filed paperwork for Java Joy, Inc., and discovered a dormant company in Texas owned the name. Before we could chase it, their trademark expired. "Sometimes someone else's trash really is your treasure," our attorney laughed.

We slapped a Vistaprint sign on a Uline janitor cart, pressed the orange cups into service, and showed up at Lorie's bank at dawn. My 4 a.m. text to Jake—"You awake?"—wasn't about supplies; it was about nerves. He replied instantly: "Let's go."

Coffee. Hug. Enjoy.

The bank lobby filled with Chamber members in suits and heels. Our Joyristas stood behind the cart in their new shirts, bright-eyed and ready. Jake poured. I straightened name tags and tried to slow my breathing.

"Coffee?" a Joyrista asked, holding out a cup. Then, with complete sincerity: "Would you like a hug?"

People laughed awkwardly. . .and then leaned in. Shoulders dropped. Eyes brightened. You could feel the room exhale. Only after the embrace did they take a sip. Somehow the coffee tasted even better.

Lorie introduced us and shared the statistic that had fueled us: eighty-seven percent of adults with disabilities who want to work can't find a job. Heads nodded. Hands reached for our "Book Us" cards. One "yes" had multiplied into dozens more.

Purpose spreads best when it is shared.

Shift the Plant

We wondered if Java Joy would work only for bank breakfasts and networking rooms. Doug, a board member who managed a manufacturing plant, offered to test that theory. His employees punched in for long shifts, grabbed earplugs and safety goggles, and kept a rhythm most of us never see. Company culture mattered to him, but he knew T-shirts don't change a soul.

Our call time was 5 a.m. We rolled the cart inside and set up next to the PPE station. Suzanne and Hannah B.—two Joyristas with Down syndrome—stood ready. Workers filed in, silent and bleary. Many were big, tattooed men, the kind you'd want on your side in a storm. Most glanced and then looked away. "Coffee?" I asked a few. "Nah," they muttered, eyes down.

My stomach sank. I leaned toward Doug. "This might have been a bad idea."

"Give it time," he said.

The first break surged at 7:15 a.m. The smell of Jittery Joe's did something our smiles hadn't yet done. A few men lined up, cups out. Hannah poured. Suzanne offered a hug. A question hovered: "A. . .hug?" They tried it like you try a new stretch—unsure, a little stiff.

One by one, the toughness faded from their bodies, replaced by easy, unrestrained grins.

By the second break, the line doubled. By the end of the morning, burly men were coming back for seconds and threes, not because the coffee had changed but because something in the room had. Doug's post-event survey came back with the highest culture ratings in a decade. People wrote things like, "Favorite day at work in years."

We talk about culture like it's a poster we can hang. But people long for joy—an honest moment to give and receive something that matters, to feel like their presence matters. Sometimes that looks like coffee. Sometimes, like a hug.

After thousands of Java Joy events, we've learned that in every room—every room—someone is personally walking the disability road:

- A mom raising a child with special needs who's afraid to talk about the appointments
- A dad working a second job so his wife can stay home with their medically fragile son
- An aunt who remembers the exact date of her nephew's diagnosis
- A friend who has watched her best friend raise a child with autism and the grief feels heavy

One in four American adults lives with a disability. For each person, there's a ring of family and friends around them, quietly carrying pieces of their story. Many of those burdens are invisible. But when a room like Java Joy shows up, something visible breaks in: connection.

Proximity builds perspective. It also resets priorities. I once complained to Joseph about yet another pair of $50 Nikes for our son. The next day, a mom told me her son had outgrown his wheelchair for the second time in two years. The cost? $25,000. Insurance would cover 70%. They owed $7,500. I haven't complained about shoe prices since.

Brené Brown says we only get a fuller picture when diverse perspectives are included, respected, and valued. I want the whole picture. Most of us do. Our brains just need help getting there.

Rewire Your Brain

We like to talk about belonging. But new belonging requires new wiring. And wiring happens through experience.

In college, my California roommate ordered guacamole. I told her I didn't like avocados. "You've never had one," she said. She was right.

I dipped a chip, rolled my eyes at myself, and took a bite. Now I would happily eat guacamole with a spoon.

That single bite formed a new neural pathway: new taste + safe friend + good laugh = "I like this." Our brains are plastic like that. Pair a comfortable something with a new experience and you carve a path that your thoughts can travel again and again.

Java Joy does that. Many guests encounter our Joyristas for the first time with a few default settings running: This might be awkward. I might say the wrong thing. Don't mess up. Then Suzanne hands them a cup. Hannah offers a hug. Laughter enters. Relief follows. A pathway is cut: This is good. I want more of this.

Most of us inherited neural maps we didn't design. We grew up rarely seeing people with disabilities included. We sat at tables with people who looked like us. Without words, we learned to look away from the man flapping his hands in the grocery store aisle. Those old paths are strong—but not sacred. They can be changed.

Children today often experience more inclusive classrooms; adults, not so much. Which means many of us will have to choose new experiences on purpose if we want new wiring.

Ask yourself: What old maps are keeping you from the blend your heart actually craves? What experience could redraw them?

Vote for a New You

James Clear says identity shifts are built on small votes: Each action is evidence for the kind of person you are becoming. Big change isn't one heroic leap; it's a thousand small "yeses."[1]

Java Joy turns rooms full of strangers into voters for joy. People show up guarded; they leave grinning. They cast a vote: I am someone who moves toward, not away. Another vote: I can talk to someone different from me and it feels. . .good. Soon the ballot box is full, and a new identity appears: a person who blends.

It happens at the intersection of problem and purpose. The problem might be "I don't know how to interact." The purpose becomes "I will learn and then model it for others."

Maybe you're a mom who wants your kids to befriend people who live differently. Maybe you're frustrated that your company's "diversity efforts" are checkboxes without connection. Maybe the word "diversity" itself makes you squirm because it feels politicized. New paths always feel awkward at first.

Remember our coffee cupping. The most popular pick was the blend. The same is true in life. We are better, stronger, fuller together—but blends take time.

A coffee bush takes roughly five years to bear fruit. Seeds become shrubs, cherries become beans, beans become cups. Good things take tending. So do movements.

What began as a janitor cart and a Kickstarter has grown tenfold—employing hundreds, serving thousands, and planting millions of small seeds of connection: one cup, one hug, one laugh at a time.

Pick Your Blend

So, what seeds are you planting?

Maybe it's inviting someone new into your small group. Maybe it's proposing a hiring process that welcomes people of all abilities. Maybe it's creating a Sunday school class for kids with sensory needs. Maybe it's simply inviting a family over whose life looks different from yours and letting the mess be part of the welcome.

Diversity cannot be outsourced to schools or HR. You get to choose your blend.

And your choice is not just about you. Neuroscientists call it *transgenerational transmission*: Our beliefs and behaviors ripple outward. The seeds we sow become shade for someone else later.

One coffee bean can grow into a plant that yields thousands of cups. Likewise, one purpose-filled idea called Java Joy has grown from a cart into a movement that's changing rooms, rewiring minds, and multiplying joy.

Because purpose is not a title; it's the change you leave in people when you do what you do. You don't need a new job to live on purpose. You need a problem that moves your heart and the willingness to bring what you already have. Dr. Patrick Hill's research adds a simple nudge: keep moving. Movement itself helps us find meaning. One of my 85-year-old mentors says the same thing without the citations: "It's easier to stay home. But if I sit still, I'll be lonely. So I keep moving." David Brooks calls it the second mountain: the one where you live for others. What if we didn't have to summit the first mountain of self before climbing the second? What if we started on the second, and let joy pull us upward?

Java Joy taught us that the blend matters. Not just in coffee, but in teams, neighborhoods, and boardrooms. The right blend isn't a sentimental poster; it's a practical advantage. It makes culture stronger and work better. It widens our vision and softens our reflexes. It opens doors—and then it holds them.

We chose a blend that day at Jittery Joe's. Ethiopian brightness. Ecuadorian sweetness. Guatemalan depth. Our Joyristas voted with coffee beans, and the room tasted what happens when difference isn't just tolerated—it's treasured.

That's the story we want every room to drink.

Coffee, Purpose, People

Our calendar filled. The bank gig turned into law firms and hospitals, startups and school systems, city halls and shop floors. We watched executives loosen their ties and tradespeople soften their shoulders. We watched people who felt invisible offer something invaluable. We watched rooms change because two worlds blended over a cup.

I still carry the image of that manufacturing plant in my back pocket for the days I forget: Suzanne reaching for men twice her size and them bending down into gentleness they didn't know they had. Hannah B. handing out hugs like medicine. Jake pouring from the same pot for the third time around, smiling like he wasn't tired at all. Doug standing off to the side, arms crossed, eyes wet.

I think of the dad who said at the bank, "We need this in our office every Monday." I think of the HR director who emailed after an event, "We planned this for morale. I didn't expect it to change me." I think of the young employee who whispered, "My daughter has Down syndrome. I've never said that at work before. Today felt safe."

You don't have to fix everything to change something. Offer a cup. Ask a name. Let a hug reset your reflex.

Keep Planting

If you want to experience joy, you have to choose a new path—one small step, one new room, one friendship at a time. Collect enough of those steps and you'll wake up blended: still yourself, but more whole.

We chose to exchange a problem for a purpose. The problem: Most adults with disabilities who want to work can't. Most workplaces don't know how to engage difference. Most of us haven't been taught how to move toward what feels unfamiliar. The purpose: Create spaces where connection happens fast and sticks—on purpose, with excellence, fueled by joy.

We are still learning. We mess up. We pour the wrong milk, run out of lids, cry in our cars after long days, and then get up and do it again because the seed is good and the soil keeps surprising us.

The word about Java Joy began to spread across Georgia. Then the seed floated farther.

And the impact of that one purpose-filled idea—the smallest seed pushed by an ordinary wind—was just beginning.

CHAPTER 15

The Hug

What Happens When We Exchange a Culture for Connection?

> *"It's wonderful to discover that what we want is not actually happiness...*
> *Joy subsumes happiness. Joy is the far greater thing."*
> —Archbishop Desmond Tutu

Head West

I was standing in my kitchen between meetings, bread in one hand and my phone in the other, when an unfamiliar San Francisco number lit up the screen. The voicemail transcription mentioned a man named Andrew who had "received a hug."

I called back.

Andrew's voice carried a Midwestern steadiness wrapped in Ivy League polish. Gifted from the start, he'd accelerated into AP classes, navigated the Ivy track, and landed on Wall Street. From there he crossed the country into venture capital—buying, building, selling tech companies and marrying Katherine, equally brilliant, equally driven. They were both in the acquiring stage of life, climbing fast.

And then came Java Joy.

He'd been in Atlanta for a global mobile-security conference, one of the board members flying in to speak. A friend and former ESP counselor, with a story that was yet to unfold, was the organizer who hired Java Joy to keep attendees fueled with caffeine. And maybe also fueled with something harder to describe. Andrew stopped by our cart for a much-needed time-zone reset.

He met Coolman first—our bald, dancing, social-media-savvy Joyrista with an ear that never fully formed and a smile that could soften granite. "Enjoy," the barista behind the cart said, eyes smiling as bright as her mouth. As Andrew scooped sugar, Coolman asked, "Want a hug?"

"A...hug?" Andrew echoed, half-amused.

"Yeah. A hug."

He said yes, awkwardly. Coolman wrapped him up, and something inside Andrew unclenched. In the middle of a polished technology conference, on the way to address thousands, he received the hug he didn't know he needed. It wasn't about helping Coolman; it was about receiving something from him that Andrew didn't even realize he was missing.

No one forgets their first Java Joy moment.

"I can't shake how I felt after Java Joy. I thought about the people back home, earbuds in, heads down, alone in their high-rises. They need this too. Could we bring Java Joy to San Francisco?"

I took a breath. Sunlight streamed through my window—the same sun that warmed him in California. Its only job was to radiate.

He was asking if we could take this little program across the country. *What if joy could radiate too?*

It felt like being 19 again, answering the call that made me a director. What stood between me and yes? The ones who were waiting, the 87 percent of adults with disabilities who want and can work but are unemployed. The Andrews of the world who don't know what they need until joy wraps its arms around them. I felt the burst activate.

"Let's do it," I said.

Three weeks later Andrew flew back to Georgia. He toured our campus, meeting Joyristas and staff, seeing the wraparound supports that make the work possible. We slid a proposal across the table, a real investment if we were going to plant this seed on the West Coast.

He didn't blink. "Let's do it."

We started planning. Friends rallied to build travel schedules; Andrew pitched Java Joy to companies in skyline buildings; we vetted coffee partners and paired with a local nonprofit to recruit unemployed adults with disabilities. Mostly, we stared at flight confirmations and grinned. Our Joyristas were about to take their first business trip.

Keep the Hug

Three days before takeoff, our nonprofit partner director in San Francisco called.

"I think we need to take out the hug," she said gently.

"The hug?" I repeated. Coffee. Hug. Enjoy. was our DNA. "Should we also take out the coffee?" I asked, half-smiling.

She didn't smile back. "Hugging feels. . .elementary. We want the Joyristas to look professional. Let's do what's appropriate."

I'd heard versions of this before. It's rarely just about a hug. It's about who decides what people need and whose comfort we're protecting. When you serve others, assumptions creep in quietly.

When we launched Java Joy, I thought of it as a training program, a chance to practice for real jobs. After a year, we asked our Joyristas, "What's your dream job?"

They stared at us.

"This is my dream job," many said, like it should have been obvious.

In the disability community, and in other marginalized groups, culture often dictates what's appropriate. But sometimes those norms are the very thing keeping us from meeting real needs.

Part of me considered giving in to the director's request. This was San Francisco. Big city. Different rules. Was it worth pushing back over something so. . .small?

Then I thought of Andrew and all the other Andrews I'd met.

We asked the Joyristas themselves: "Hug or no hug?"

"People need hugs," Hannah said without hesitation.

"They love our hugs," Suzanne added.

Nicky shrugged. "Not everybody. That's okay—high-fives or air hugs for them."

Decision made.

Yes, hugging in business can be tricky. Which is why we train for it. Joyristas learn to ask, to accept "no" cheerfully, to offer alternatives, and to hug appropriately when it's welcomed. The point isn't to force a moment; it's to offer one. Awkward often opens the door to aha. Then aha moments often rewire us.

The Dalai Lama said, "When we are born, there is no formality. When we die, there is no formality. Formality is artificial; it just creates additional barriers." Our teams, our families, our communities are starving for leaders willing to remove barriers, even if it makes people shift in their seats.

I told our partner, kindly but clearly, "The hug stays—by consent, with training, and always with alternatives. A hug from a Joyrista is 100% authentic. It's human. And humans need it."

Eat the Biscoff

Friday arrived. Four of our original Georgia Joyristas met us at the building.

- Nicky, the self-proclaimed Coffee Fairy
- Hannah, our singing extraordinaire
- Colin, the one and only Coolman
- Megan, our baker beauty

Our goal was bigger than bookings. We were going to train the 11 adults with disabilities we'd hired in San Francisco to become Joyristas for the Bay Area. Our traveling band included the Joyristas, a videographer, three staff, one board chair, insulin shots, behavior plans, spare glasses, and enough Java Joy swag to turn Terminal F into a parade.

We brought tiny ground coffee bags with a note on it sharing who we were to hand to passengers at the gate. "We're headed to San Francisco to spread joy," we explained. "Apologies in advance if your flight is. . .*rowdier* than usual." The videographer stretched across an aisle midflight to get the shot. Passengers laughed and filmed us filming them.

And then there were the Biscoff cookies.

By hour four, the Joyristas had professed their love for those caramelized biscuits at least a dozen times. A flight attendant appeared at their row holding a shrink-wrapped case—100 cookies. He turned to me with tears in his eyes and whispered that his nephew has autism.

Watching our Joyristas flying across the country to work gave him hope for his nephew's future. The hugs he received in exchange were extra.

When we landed, another flight attendant took the intercom. "Joyristas, on behalf of Delta and all the passengers on this flight, it was a *joy* having you on our flight. Go spread hugs all over San Francisco."

The cabin erupted. People asked for hugs on the way out. "Start with us—we need one!"

And spread hugs they did.

San Francisco, Meet Joy

From Transamerica to Goldman Sachs, from Lyft to Airbnb, joy ricocheted off glass towers that week. Our Athens crew worked shoulder-to-shoulder with the 11 new Bay Area hires. The first morning was all nerves; by afternoon, they were moving like a team that had been together for years.

That's when we met John.

Six-foot-six and broad-shouldered, John's awkward smile and bright eyes were the first things I noticed. His job coach had been looking for the right fit for a long time. Within hours, John stood on a downtown sidewalk doing a live interview for Channel 2 while also spotting customers. "Excuse me, sir! Free coffee and joy!" "Ma'am, good morning! Would you like a free hug?"

By midweek, his coach found me. "John's been let go from job after job for being 'too'—too loud, too kind, too enthusiastic, too much. Watching him at your cart...it's like he was born to be a Joyrista."

What began as a way to let strangers taste the Joy Exchange in little Watkinsville, Georgia, was changing lives on the other side of the country. Java Joy had become a portal, perfectly positioning adults with disabilities in jobs designed for their strengths, doing something I, and many others, were not designed to do: be a Joyrista.

John still talks with the Georgia crew regularly—time zones and distance be forgotten. During the pandemic, that connection saved him. Community is borderless when joy is the language.

Let the Fairy Fly

One of our midweek bookings took us high into a JP Morgan Chase tower. Bankers streamed in, many returning for second and third cups (and who could blame them?).

Nicky—the Coffee Fairy—floated through the office taking names and orders. At first glance, you saw a tall, commanding Black man with cornrows beaded in seashells and the characteristics of autism. Watch him for five minutes, and you saw more: flair, memory, presence, a knack for names and recipes, and a natural authority to light up a room. His abilities activated.

Near the end of the booking, an older white gentleman pulled me aside. He had the practical questions—How does this work? Who pays for what?—but something else pressed behind his eyes.

"How was your experience?" I asked.

He leaned in, shoulder brushing mine, eyes suddenly wet. The words surprised him as they fell out: "I haven't had a hug in five years."

After a divorce, with grown kids scattered, the absence of touch had become his normal. Nicky's all-encompassing embrace cracked something open. He left with a promise to donate funds that would underwrite more employment hours we couldn't cover with bookings alone.

Joy exchanged: a man unknowingly starved for connection, a Joyrista eager to give it. Both left fuller.

He is not alone.

Avoidance of physical connection has been trending for decades. Tech replaces in-person conversations. We live in silos. Abuse statistics make risk managers throw the baby out with the bathwater. A global pandemic trains us to doubt every hand we brush.

Anthropologists note that Western culture is the most touch-deprived in the world. Have we drifted too far from something our bodies were made for?

The Science—and Sense—of a Hug

Psychologist Dacher Keltner has spent years studying human touch. Everyday gestures—a pat on the back, a brief arm squeeze—are easy to dismiss, but they are profound carriers of compassion. Touch is a primary language of connection. It's also good for health. Another study found that eight hugs a day are the baseline for mental stability, while 12 lead us to emotional growth.[1]

At ESP, many of our Joyristas never unlearned this language. Their five-year-old selves never left. They greet with proximity and warmth, without apologies.

Perhaps you grew up in a family that wasn't physically affectionate. Maybe trauma made touch feel unsafe. The hopeful news: The brain is malleable. Positive emotions like compassion are skills we can practice. With appropriate training and consent, we can relearn good touch.

So ask yourself:

- Who in your life needs your touch?
- What might a quick shoulder squeeze do for an employee who's quietly carrying too much?
- What could become of regular hugs with your friends?
- And the next time you see someone in need. . .would a handshake, fist bump, or air hug be the better first gift than a lecture or a link?

The goal isn't to turn your office into a cuddle party. It's to tell the truth with our bodies: You matter, I see you, you belong.

Iron the Apron

We ended the San Francisco launch with a moment I still carry in my bones—the White Apron Ceremony.

All week our Bay Area trainees had worn blue aprons labeled training. Now, on a rooftop overlooking downtown, the Athens crew stood beside them. One by one, our original Joyristas stepped forward, named an ability they had seen come alive—a laugh that disarmed a room, a memory for names, a steady hand on the carafe—and slipped a crisp white apron over a new teammate's head. Names were embroidered across each chest like a promise.

Parents cried big, happy tears that had been waiting for years. Their adult children had been seen before. But this was something different: seen, celebrated, and launched.

This entire ceremony existed because Andrew received a hug from Coolman in a hotel lobby and chose not to keep it to himself. True joy refuses to stay in one place.

Repeat It

Not long after that trip, we served coffee at a statewide leadership gathering. The keynote was from the CEO of one of the largest restaurant chains in America. He was supposed to head straight to get mic'd. Instead, he stopped at the cart.

He took his coffee, answered the question of the day ("What do you hope to get for Christmas?"), and received a hug. "A hug, huh," he said, grinning. Then he squeezed behind the cart next to Coolman and started serving.

Here was a man who understood service. In one unscripted move, the line between "us" and "them" disappeared. Six months later, that same leader—Dan Cathy—championed Java Joy for the Chick-fil-A True Inspiration Award. The funding helped us imagine growing more carts, and more hugs, to more cities.

Dan often says, "Repetition yields constants, and constants create cultures." Java Joy's constant—Coffee. Hug. Enjoy.—isn't gimmick; it's formation. Do something small and good often enough, and people begin to trust it. Do it long enough, and culture shifts around it.

We think we're chasing happiness. What we're actually starving for is joy, the kind that arrives when we trade the safety of our current culture for the courage to connect.

Our culture says: Keep your head down. Be efficient. Don't risk awkward. Guard the edges. Our souls say: Look up. Be human. Risk awkward. Cross the room.

Our culture says: Keep it professional. Our bodies say: Please, just one real sign that I belong.

I'm not naïve. Boundaries matter; consent matters. The hug stays because those also matter. And because we have learned to ask first, offer alternatives, and honor "no," the "yes" that follows carries weight. The embrace becomes a chosen connection that people remember months later, on an elevator ride, when everything feels sharp and silent and they need to recall a moment when it didn't.

Let It

A hug launched Java Joy in San Francisco. A hug handed a flight attendant hope for his nephew. A hug rewired a banker who hadn't felt human touch in five years. A hug invited a CEO to cross the counter and join the joy club. A hundred small hugs turned into white aprons on a rooftop and paid hours of meaningful work for adults who had been told they were "too" something for too long.

Not every city will welcome the Java Joy hugs. Not every room will want them. That's okay. But where it is offered and received, it opens a door. The awkward becomes aha. The stranger becomes a neighbor. Culture becomes connection.

If You're Wondering What to Do
You don't need a cart to change a room. You need a posture.

- Ask. "Would you like a hug, a handshake, a high-five, or an air hug?" Let people choose their way in.
- Adjust. If they say no, honor it gladly. Connection without consent is not connection.
- Appreciate. When someone says yes, receive it. Let it tell the truth your head forgot: You are not alone.

If touch isn't yours to give right now, offer something else embodied: your full attention, your eye contact, your Friday afternoon walk to the parking lot with someone who always walks alone, your "How did it go?" after their doctor's appointment. There are a thousand ways to put skin on welcome.

Choose Joy, the Far Greater Thing
Back in my kitchen, long after that first phone call, I thought again about what Archbishop Tutu said: Happiness is lovely, but "joy is the far greater thing." Happiness flares and fades. Joy roots and radiates. It grows when we exchange the culture we inherited for the connection we are made for.

What could your hug do?

Don't wait five years.

Take a page from Nicky and John, from Coolman, Hannah, and Megan. Take a page from your own book—the one you wrote when you were five.

Go hug someone, if they will accept one. Let the awkward lead to an aha moment. Call an invisible reality into an invaluable light. Let connection activate something in you and in the person you touch.

Then watch joy—quiet, stubborn, far-greater joy—unfold.

In a world built to keep us efficient and apart, the simplest human exchange might be the most revolutionary: Coffee. Hug. Enjoy.

CHAPTER **16**

The Spread

What Happens When We Exchange Moments for Movements?

> "Joy is the reward, really, of seeking to give joy to others."
> —The Dalai Lama

Catch It If You Can

Courtesy of a global pandemic, you may still twitch at the words *contagious* or *spread*. It can feel too soon to use such terms, maybe always will. And yet the past few years handed us a common language: We now understand, viscerally, how something small can move through a room, then a city, and then a country, reshaping how everyone lives, works, and relates.

The question is whether we'll associate that kind of momentum only with harm or whether we'll harness it for good. Because like it or not, something is always spreading. The power is ours to decide what moves through our homes, our businesses, and our communities.

Long before I could name it, I was watching another kind of contagion at work. From San Francisco skyscrapers to a car dealership on the edge of town, people were catching on: Joy spreads, too.

Barbara, our beautifully direct, unfiltered friend who hosted The Night That Could Change It All, felt the joy and immediately moved it forward. She had a regular gig at Bulldog Kia, filming commercials in her famous drawl: "We'll see ya—at Bulldog Kia!" (If you read that without a Georgia accent, try again.) She couldn't get over Java Joy or Coolman, who delighted in parroting her tagline.

Barbara knew up close how hard employment could be for people with disabilities; as you now know, her grandson Matthew has cerebral palsy. She also knew, as only a grandmother can, how much ability lives inside the label. One afternoon, sitting in her glass-walled prayer room, I shared our next practical hurdle: If we wanted Java Joy to serve more places, we needed vehicles to tow our new concession trailers.

Barbara didn't blink. She called the owners David and James on the spot and booked us a meeting for the next day. There, we told them about ESP, about Big Hearts, about Java Joy. They listened, grinned, and asked the magic question: "How can we help?" Days later, they agreed to our bold ask: two vehicles for our trailers in exchange for Java Joy serving at the dealership every Friday.

The first Friday didn't feel like a corporate activation. It felt like a family reunion where not everyone knew they were related yet. Hugs happened. Stories surfaced. Customers started lingering, then returning. Employees came early on Fridays and stayed late. Before long, the joyristas were making cameos with Barbara in commercials, and Bulldog Kia pledged proceeds from each sale to ESP.

One December afternoon, auditing operations, I turned a corner and stopped cold. A Joyrista was doing a Christmas gift exchange with one of the technicians—a middle-aged Caucasian mechanic and an African American man with a disability, laughing over inside jokes the rest of us weren't in on. It wasn't staged. It was friendship. That's what the joy had done: made the unlikely feel inevitable.

I hustled to David's office to brag on his team. Before I could start, he waved a hand. "Laura, Java Joy is the best thing we've done for our business. Sales are up over the last two months, but best of all, my employees love being here on Fridays. They don't want to miss. The joyristas are part of the team."

The spread wasn't just wide. Now it was deep.

And it kept going. James, one of the owners, walked through a challenging divorce. Friday joy became a lifeline. Months later at Big Hearts he met Charlotte, a mama to Claudia—brown curly hair, kinetic energy, never forgets a name—with autism. James and Charlotte bonded on the dance floor and married two years later. James later told us he never would've imagined such a scenario unfolding in his life, marrying someone with a child with a disability. But Java Joy changed what he saw as possible. It expanded his capacity to see, embrace, and love. The joy spread inside him, and everything shifted.

What I was witnessing in real time has a name: emotional contagion. Teams catch feelings. One person's posture ripples outward, nudging a room toward cynicism or collaboration. Studies show positive emotion spreads especially fast in cooperative groups; shared laughter, gratitude, delight—they pull people forward together. That's what I saw at the dealership: customers lingering, co-workers helping, owners softening, lives realigned.

Joy is not passive. It's persuasive.

Let It Move

The spread reached people who had been around ESP for years and still found themselves undone by a new encounter. Duke and Tammy Lindsay are "make-it-happen" people—country-club polished and Christmas-Eve-with-a-moving-truck gritty. As owners of a local moving company, they could get anything from point A to point B. That year, they discovered something else could be moved.

At a Java Joy pop-up in a salon, I watched Tammy and her daughter, Kaeti, step into the line. Kaeti glowed—newly married, hand often on her small, rounding belly. I assumed they were there for haircuts. And then Suzanne, our artist Joyrista whose smile could outshine the sun, reached for their cups. Hannah followed with a hug. I watched Tammy's whole body soften. Tears welled; the hugs lingered.

When they reached me, Kaeti placed a hand on her stomach. "We just found out our little girl—her name is Wynnie—has Down syndrome." Tears spilled when she said the name. I kissed that belly without thinking, feeling an unexplainable homecoming to a person I hadn't met yet.

"I don't fear what life will look like," she said, glancing back at Suzanne and Hannah. "Watching them gives me so much hope. They bring joy. I feel blessed that we've been given that same joy in our family."

Wynnie arrived like a spark. In the seven years since, she has danced through camps and across grocery-store aisles, hugging half the town and galvanizing the other half with sheer delight. The Lindsays learned what many of us have: joy doesn't stay where you found it. It moves person to person, house to house, generation to generation.

The only question is whether we'll be brave enough to keep it moving.

When the Wrong Thing Spreads

The month we launched Java Joy in San Francisco—a business built on hugs—was the same month an invisible virus called COVID-19 began quietly spreading there. Weeks later, the city shut down. Our West Coast operation stopped. Flights canceled. Contracts paused. Joy felt like a luxury word.

Back home, we scrambled. We kept our Joyristas on payroll and pivoted. "Joy Starters" kicked off virtual company meetings with dance parties. Friends purchased "Joyrgrams"—video messages from Joyristas—so people isolated on birthdays or battling illness knew they were not alone.

Our other ESP programs morphed into phone chains and emergency support. Staff dressed in costumes and spaced themselves a parking spot apart to host drive-through parades. I stood at the end of the line with a muumuu and a sign—"You've got this"—and wondered privately if we had this.

That summer, with schools closed and families hanging by a thread, we did the impossible: six summer camps, simultaneously, in six different locations. We learned a lot about spread—college students occasionally forget rules, and viruses like friendship. But something else moved faster: resilience, resourcefulness, kinship.

If we could do six camps in six towns, we could do this anywhere.

Not long after, we were hosting one of the state's first vaccination events—complete with music therapists, cookies shaped like suns, and banners that read, "Here Comes the Sun." It sounds small. It wasn't. Even in a pandemic, we could choose joy. Not as a denial of reality, but as the practice of seeing and being seen. And when joy shows up in a season like that, it does what it always does: It spreads.

We had lived through what happens when fear spreads. Now we could show what happens when joy does.

Spread to the Westside

A year earlier, a family named Dempsey had visited our campus. After watching flag circle, they stood in tears. "Either we're moving here," they said, "or we're bringing ESP home."

At the time, it felt impossible. After the Great Summer of Six, I called them. "I think we can do it," I said. "Let's start with Java Joy. We just figured out six camps in six locations. This is our chance."

"Use us as the experiment," Gaines Dempsey said through tears. "We'll do whatever it takes."

They did. They galvanized their town, rallied friends, and told a new story about what belonging could look like on the west side of our state. Today, hundreds of people in Northwest Georgia are tasting ESP—camp rhythms, club nights, Java Joy Fridays. We're building a campus and walking the same slow, sacred process of watching a community change as it makes space for all.

Spread to the Center

Around the same time, my friend Chad was itching to bring Java Joy to Atlanta. In truth, he was part of what got us to San Francisco in the first place—he was the friend that booked us for the technology conference where we met Andrew. But Chad's story started long before that, with a bowling lane and a little matchmaking.

Years ago, I slid tiny, sweet, bright Kim into a lane with Chad who was spunky, loud, full of life. They were meant to be. By August they were suntanned and smitten, tubing the Chattahoochee with their ESP friends—summer love formed through shared service.

A year later, Chad led Kim back to where they met. On the porch of the ESP gym, he slipped a ring on her finger. Months after that, they walked down the aisle with ESP friends as ring-bearers and flower girls.

Then, a message from Kim. Their firstborn had been diagnosed at three months with a chromosomal deletion. They were suddenly on the other side of our mission. She ended with a sentence most new parents don't have: *We know where to turn.* They had a community waiting with open arms.

When their son Hayes turned four, the circle closed. "He's four—can he come to camp?" they asked. They walked into our new building for the parent meeting, amazed by the resources and somehow totally at home. Once family, always family. After-school buddies who were campers a decade earlier greeted them like they'd just stepped out for a snack.

Watching bright-eyed, red-haired Hayes chase joy across the gym, I flashed back to that summer a dozen years prior, to that porch engagement, to a "perfect little human" now surrounded by ESP love and thought: meant to be.

Chad became the person who booked unbookable rooms in Atlanta—statewide chambers, legislative breakfasts, global conferences. He and our Leadership Georgia friends, the Edmonds, joined forces, and within a year we'd hired 20 Joyristas, launched a permanent cart inside Mercedes-Benz Stadium, and started serving some of downtown's most iconic companies.

Atlanta's Java Joy now fuels summer camps and club nights in Marietta. Volunteers like my best friend Jenni—a CHOA NICU nurse by day, overnight camp nurse by summer—are stitching together a community that looks and feels like Northeast and Northwest Georgia: joyful, interdependent, sticky. Emotional contagion is not a metaphor here; it's a method. Fear or hope. Isolation or belonging. Cynicism or contagious joy. Communities don't drift toward joy; people choose it and carry it.

Our vision reaches beyond Georgia. Think Boys & Girls Clubs or Habitat for Humanity—familiar names that mean "you're welcome here" in any ZIP code. We imagine a world where more communities experience contagious joy through programs with people of all abilities, with Java Joy leading the way in workplaces.

Journeys of Joy

The quick jaunt to San Francisco taught us that joy is needed everywhere—and it taught us a life lesson I didn't see coming. Plenty of people travel for work. But if you carry a disability diagnosis, you may not have a job, let alone the chance to travel for it. That first trip told our Georgia Joyristas something their bodies never forget: Your gifts are needed elsewhere. Your joy is portable. . .and valuable.

So when our first invitation arrived to serve an HR conference in Austin, we said yes. Then Denver. Miami. San Diego. We coined the term Journeys of Joy and learned to pack like professionals—uniforms, sleeves, stickers, the "Hug Counter," and a simple checklist texted to Joyristas before each trip:

- Shoes you can stand in
- Snacks you can share
- Hugs you can offer (if they say yes)

One Journey of Joy ended at my friend Mark's IT company holiday party. Ugly sweaters, hot chocolate, and a CEO who believes joy at work is a strategy, not a perk. We hired a few local adults with disabilities for that event—meaningful income, meaningful role, right where they live. We left behind what we always hope to leave: an afterglow of exchanged joy, a room full of rewired assumptions, and one persistent question: "How could we employ someone like this here?"

Journeys of Joy help fund the everyday. Java Joy is a social enterprise; the revenue we earn helps underwrite the programs our Joyristas love taking PTO for—like "adult camp," where sorority and fraternity parties are reimagined with root beer and early bedtimes. A joy shared truly is a joy doubled.

Spread Over the Pond

One of our most unexpected journeys started with a phone call and ended with hundreds of people receiving a gift they didn't know they wanted.

Marci—a spunky real-estate leader with a reflex for problem-solving—had booked Java Joy for a large Atlanta event. She called one day with an unusual invitation. She'd met a refined, generous

British woman helping her sons start a charitable foundation in the United States. Marci had pitched Java Joy because it matched their values. "They want to underwrite a Joyrista salary for a year," she said. "Maybe two."

I was thrilled—and curious. "Who are her sons?"

"Keep this low," she whispered. "He's filming nearby. It's Tom Holland."

I did what any nearly-40 mother who only watches rom-coms would do: I Googled. That night, over dinner where we each share one joy from the day, one junkie thing and one way we saw Jesus that day. . .I announced my joy: a potential donation from an actor's family to support Java Joy. "Who?" my kids asked.

"Tom Holland," I said. "Apparently he's Spider-Man."

My children looked at me like I'd confessed I didn't know what pizza is. "Mom," Owen sighed, "you don't know Tom Holland?" "Zendaya's boyfriend!" Finley added. Even #lovelikeJoseph smirked. (If I went to more movies with him, we wouldn't be in this situation.)

A video call with Tom's mom, Nikki, followed. In her lilting accent she shared the heart of The Brothers Trust and offered to underwrite two Joyristas for a year. I introduced our crew and couldn't resist the symmetry: With her name Nikki, perhaps she'd like to fund Nicky, our Coffee Fairy. She loved it. The second Joyrista would be our first Atlanta hire, Liz.

Their support grew—two Joyristas, then three, then four—as the foundation expanded and their hearts stretched with it. In year three, Nikki said, "Would a Journey of Joy to London be possible? We're hosting a gala in March. I'd love your Joyristas there."

Say less.

I called Carter and Kim—always game for an adventure—and invited Chris and Brittany, dear friends whose Loverly Grey platform had been quietly spreading, and they could not help but use their spotlight to shine it on ESP. But, this trip would become a turning point for them, too.

We loaded up Nicky and Liz, Alex from our team, too many bags, and enough flair to be flagged by TSA twice. Carter filled the itinerary with West End shows and good food. Highlights: Liz trying sushi with Brittany cheering her on; Nicky's hunt for every candy shop within a 3-mile radius; a proper High Tea where we sat and sipped for four hours; and *Frozen* on stage. At the moment Elsa transformed, Nicky shot to his feet and boomed, "Oh my goodness! Beautiful!" The audience gasped, then laughed, then stood—with him, because joy is contagious and theater etiquette is no match for wonder.

And then the gala—the Brothers Trust Ball. If you remember the story at the book's beginning, this was the night of the *Titanic* moment: Nicky and Tom Holland on stage, singing "My Heart Will Go On," striking the iconic pose as if the West End were their living room. It was outrageous and perfect.

That night stamped something into my bones: Across oceans and accents, joy is the same language.

Hard-Wire for Joy

Developmental researcher Allan Schore calls joy the key ingredient in early social development.[1] We are, quite literally, wired for connection. And while those first months matter, the research is equally clear about our brains across a lifetime: They're malleable. Jim Wilder describes it as a "joy capacity" we can grow—practices and people that expand our ability to receive and give delight.[2]

Some folks radiate joy more naturally—like comedians who can make almost anything funny. But some jokes land no matter who tells them. Joy works that way, too. Yes, our Joyristas carry a higher baseline of joy than anyone I've ever met; they're confident in their skin, lead with an ability filter, and lean toward compassion. Yet every one of us can learn their way. We can raise our capacity.

At 18, I didn't know that I'd spend my career sitting at the feet of joy experts. I didn't know I'd grow by watching them. That is, in many ways, why I'm writing this book—so you can borrow my front-row seat. I've watched people lose their capacity for joy as they age. I've also watched our members—through obstacles, diagnoses, and years—carry joy like a pilot light that never goes out.

You can cultivate that, too.

Let It Stick

Joy is contagious—but it becomes culture only if we let it. As neighbors, parents, leaders, and teammates, we each shape the emotional climate of our spaces. Look around: People with disabilities and their authentic, unfiltered joy are gaining cultural ground. You can see it in shows like *Love on the Spectrum*, in businesses like Bitty & Beau's Coffee, and in countless small moments you'll never see on a screen: a Joyrista remembering a customer's name and order, a banker realizing he hasn't been hugged in five years, a grandmother deciding a car dealership can be a community center on Fridays.

We all long for joy. And when it shows up, we lean in. That's emotional contagion. That's the quiet power your life already holds.

So how do we keep it moving?

- Pay attention to the climate you create. Do people breathe easier around you—or brace?
- Lean into the awkward. The first hug, the first hello, the first "Tell me about your child"—it all feels clumsy before it becomes natural.
- Choose proximity. Sit closer. Ask the second question. Stay five more minutes.

Be intentional about who you let influence your emotional weather. Emotions are contagious. Surround yourself with people like Nicky and Liz—people whose joy radiates effortlessly—and your odds of catching it (and passing it on) go way up.

Take the Wider View

A dealership changed its Fridays. A moving company moved more than furniture. A chamber breakfast rewired a room. A rooftop in London erupted into song. A stadium in Atlanta served more than coffee. A pandemic tried to isolate us, and we found new ways to say, "Here comes the sun."

Seed by seed, hug by hug, city by city—joy traveled. Every time someone received it and then gave it away, it multiplied. That's the math of the Joy Exchange.

We've already seen what happens when the wrong thing spreads. We carry those losses together. Now we get to decide what spreads next.

Let it be joy. Then we can carry the wins together.

CHAPTER 17

The Miracle

What Happens When We Exchange Silos for Shared Spaces?

> *"There is no joy in possession without sharing."*
> —Desiderius Erasmus

Trust the Rookie

As ESP expanded into new communities and joy leapt borders, something just as profound was happening at home. Our own town was quietly transforming beneath our feet. Joy was reaching wide, yes, but it was also seeping deep—into hidden corners, softening hard places, illuminating the darker crevices where people felt alone. That's the quiet power of joy: It doesn't just travel; it transforms.

Jonah walked into my office with that brand of conviction only a college-athlete-turned-intern can carry. He had discovered a recreational sports program for people with disabilities and came armed with a typed proposal and a glossy pamphlet. His plan was simple and hopeful. It was exactly the kind of dream I would've sketched at 19: a baseball field, a program, a few thousand dollars to make it happen.

He had no idea what it would truly take. Neither did I at his age. And who was I to stifle a dream, especially one dreamed for others?

As I read the proposal, my mind drifted to my ring bearer turned co-worker—Dakota—now a Joyrista with blue eyes, a sports brain, and a taste for mischief. He grew up with his wheelchair pressed to the chain-link fence while his brother played travel ball. Their home was team central on weekends—teenagers tossing balls in the yard, teasing Dakota, flipping through his stack of ESP photos. His mom, a nurse with a deep well of tenderness, and his dad, Joe—a paramedic-turned-nurse—poured everything into their boys, their sports, and Georgia athletics.

Joe also carried one quiet dream: to coach Dakota, too.

I sent one exploratory email to a national contact and braced for the usual waiting game. Minutes later, an answer blinked in:

"Laura, it's so great to hear from you. You may not realize this, but Miracle League, which now has more than 300 fields, started in Georgia. I just moved my family to Watkinsville where ESP is, and I've been hoping someone there would take on a project in this area. Everyone keeps telling me about ESP. This must be a God thing. When can I visit?"

One visit and one board strategy session later, we knew: This wasn't just a good idea. It was the next right project.

We learned the newest Miracle League communities weren't stopping at baseball diamonds; they were pairing fields with universally designed playgrounds so kids with and without disabilities could play side by side. The playground manufacturer had become a research leader in inclusive play. Their data affirmed what we'd always suspected: When a typically developing child plays freely with a child who has a disability—without barriers, without labels—that first connection often lays a lifelong neural pathway toward inclusion.

Positive experiences create positive connections. Repeated, they become reflex.

With Java Joy, we were rewiring adult perceptions at the office coffee cart. With this project, we could shape how children begin to see one another, before fear or unfamiliarity writes its first draft.

Imagine a cohort of kids growing up already seeing their peers with disabilities as friends, teammates, and neighbors who are fully capable, fully valued.

The Miracle 169

Research fueled our resolve. Then Mariah told me she hadn't set foot on a playground since the brain tumor changed her childhood. Pair that with Joe's hope to coach Dakota, and it didn't feel like a project; it felt like a calling. We launched a multimillion-dollar campaign and drafted the footprint we hoped would anchor future ESP locations:

- A Miracle League field for recreational play
- A universally designed "Playground of Possibilities" for all abilities
- A snack stand that created meaningful employment

There are playgrounds everywhere. But the difference between ordinary and extraordinary is just a little extra. For us, extra meant designing every inch so every child could play.

Our big idea inflated Jonah's "few thousand" into "several million." Time to build a team.

Make No Small Plans
To win, we needed City Hall. Our land was a patchwork—part city, part VFW (thanks to our beloved Dave the hog farmer). As it turned out, the mayor was another Big-Hearted Dave.

Mayor Dave was a vibrant character in our small Georgia town. He and his partner, Mario, ran the local bed-and-breakfast. A Boston native with creative director credentials, he brought color to everything: Hawaiian shirts, a wide-angle grin, and a knack for curating weddings and concerts that stitched people together. He was a regular at ESP—coffee in hand, middle of the morning flag circle, soaking up hugs. Beneath the loud shirts was his superpower: vision. He could see what didn't exist yet and talk about it as if it already did.

On a hot August afternoon, I laid renderings on his desk: research on inclusive play, Miracle League designs, rough budgets, 100 tiny hurdles: council votes, public feedback, permits, city dollars. We dreamed. Then reality would creep in—construction costs, timelines, terrain challenges. I caught myself scaling back.

Dave leaned across the desk—salt-and-pepper hair falling across his forehead, one button too casual—and put his hand over mine. "Laura," he said quietly, "make no small plans."

It became his refrain. He said it through the fall, through budget meetings, and again in wintry Minnesota, where Councilman Brian, Dave, and I tried zip lines on icy equipment and made snow angels like kids on a field trip. "Make no small plans," he'd grin, "and make them here."

With Dave's vision and a steady council, the early hurdles fell: city support, votes cast, permits in motion. Opposition surfaced (of course it did), but Dave refused to be distracted. He tuned out the noise, stayed on the goal, and kept clearing the path.

Midway through the process, Dave was diagnosed with cancer. He never saw the project completed.

Now, every time I cross our property, past a playground roaring with laughter and a Miracle League field humming with joy, I think of him. Of his belief. Of his boldness. Of the man who took Jonah's bold proposal and my scaled-down sketches and gave them a sky.

Make no small plans.

Break the Silos

At first our plan felt like a guaranteed home run. Then we remembered: Not everyone loves baseball. And not everyone loves change. Most of the community rallied, but pockets resisted. A few argued, quite literally, that trees deserved to stand more than children with disabilities deserved a place to play.

The deeper we dug—figuratively and with backhoes—the more pushback we met. Neighbors worried about traffic and noise. Our new mayor (I'll call him Bill) became an outspoken critic. Thankfully, council stayed steady. They hosted open forums so residents could study designs, chat with architects, ask hard questions, and be heard.

And then there was. . .let's call her Karen (it just fits). Every town has one. She came armed with binders thick as Bibles—meeting minutes, budgets, highlighter fireworks. Our team made a lighthearted game of guessing how many times she'd speak or how long she'd delay the agenda. Month after month, Karen opposed not just us but any change. I often wondered what might happen if she poured all that energy into building instead of blocking. What a force she'd be.

Her resistance crystallized something for me. We all face the same daily choice: build silos that keep us apart or create spaces that bring us together.

I remembered the ant colony unit from third grade. Ants are natural architects of connection. Colonies expand, they adapt, and when they encounter a gap, they don't build higher walls; they make bridges. If a height difference threatens access, they form ramps—living ones—so everyone reaches food and shelter.

That is asset-based community development (ABCD) in motion: Identify the strengths you already have and link them in ways that multiply impact. We already had families, kids, volunteers, donors, city leaders. What we lacked was a shared space to braid them together.

Innovation looks inspiring on a website. In real life, it disrupts habits: A few trees come down, a Tuesday night gets spent at council, a budget flexes so the whole town can flourish. Dismantling silos costs comfort. In our case, the cost was about to show up both above and below ground.

Midseason Trades

As the "pouring concrete instead of saving trees" rhetoric heated up, our excavators hit rock under those very trees. Post-COVID construction costs were spiking. Our budget was ballooning. Tempers flared at meetings. Odds felt stacked against us.

It was kind of like the 2021 Atlanta Braves. Midseason, they had a losing record, a superstar sidelined, key players gone, and a sliver of a chance at a title. Everyone wrote them off. Then came a handful of midseason trades—quiet, decisive reinforcements—and everything changed. By October, they were World Series champions.

So you're saying there's a chance.

Our midseason reinforcements didn't wear cleats. They wore name badges.

Sharyn, our city manager, worked like Charlotte in *Charlotte's Web*—quick, principled, and precise—spinning a hedge of protection around a fragile idea. Aligned with a steady council, she shepherded process and kept politics from swallowing purpose.

Not long after, the mayor resigned, and the mayor *pro tem* stepped up. Brian, a hometown son, believed our town could be both charming and forward-thinking. He was strong, clear, and immune to drama.

Then came Ross—Rosie's dad—who joined as our contractor so we could stop bleeding dollars through a large firm. For Ross and his wife, Cathy, the project was personal: a tribute to Rosie, with something special planned for the final installation. He was a close friend of Joe—Dakota's dad—who tragically died from COVID-19 while serving as a medic, a job that he knew put him in the crosshairs of the virus nearly every day. He served anyway. Ross, along with parents like Jason and Christy, carried Joe's dream forward with fierce tenderness.

The team expanded beyond parents and city staff. Coaches of local baseball teams opened their fields so we could share the vision and pass the hat. Players and families baked and sold brookies (brownie-cookie hybrids) to raise funds. Elementary and middle schoolers became "Lemonade Leaders," working at stands to learn leadership, volunteerism, and abilities awareness while contributing their quarters.

A hometown family stepped up to the plate. The mom, once an ESP counselor who took a chance on me in my first year, later faced the silence of infertility after her first child. They could have stayed siloed but instead opened their home to foster children. Once staff and now an ESP mom, she carried a simple dream: that her son with autism might one day round the bases. That dream gave her the energy to join our team and cheer the Miracle into being.

Family foundations stepped in. Among them were friends of another Matthew. Tall, blue-eyed, spiky-haired, with a gregarious grin, Matthew has autism. Before ESP, public spaces overwhelmed him; headphones were mandatory, meltdowns common. Years later, he was leading songs at flag circle. His transformation moved those friends to partially fund the Playground of Possibilities.

A plaque on its side bears the words that steadied me through more than one long night:

> "Jesus looked at them and said, 'With man this is impossible, but with God all things are possible.'"

Piece by piece, our roster formed. The team wasn't just our board and the families we serve. It had become the city, the schools, the neighbors—the whole town choosing to move from mine to ours. From them to us.

That is how both championships and community miracles are built—not by star players alone but by a team willing to keep moving forward together when the odds say don't.

Expect the Extraordinary

Opening day finally arrived, on the doorstep of summer camp. Invitations sent, RSVPs tallied. We set up a baseball-card-signing reception where Miracle League players handed out their own cards. The concession stand served cupcakes, Cracker Jacks, popcorn, popsicles, cotton candy. We were equal parts county fair and holy day.

Clipboard in hand, I worked the checklists.

A young girl and her family arrived early. "Could we try the playground?" they asked, fingers wrapped around the fence. I opened the gate. She leaned toward me; I lifted her and carried her into the Playground of Possibilities. She crawled, her AFO leg braces scraping the ramp, and then pulled herself up and pushed her walker across the first play panel designed for her. One by one, she tried every element—ramping, spinning, sliding—no back door, no "you can't."

Then came Wynnie—now five—toddling with her little brother through the gate. My own five-year-old, Tate, tore past like a comet and then circled back to climb beside them. For a moment I just stood there: Wynnie's giggle, Tate's yell, a new camper's walker wheels clicking rhythm, parents with hands over mouths as if they'd stumbled onto a miracle.

Because they had.

More than 1,000 people, ESP families, and community members and families joined us for opening day. We hosted the first pitch in honor of Joe, the medic, Dakota's dad, who helped imagine the project but never got to see it in fruition. Dakota caught the first ball. And then we unveiled the secret project Ross and I, along with his team, had been quietly working on. A monument, with a bronze girl in a wheelchair on top, coming out of her chair and reaching for the sky, holding a butterfly. Below her, the names of the ESP friends we lost to soon. Our very own Angels in the Outfield memorial. Parents wept. Their child not forgotten, still welcome.

Three years of council meetings, donations, sleepless nights, and literal rock felt more than worth it. It was perfect—not because nothing was missing but because everyone was present.

Perfection isn't the absence of things. It's the presence of belonging. And here, everyone belonged. *That* was the miracle.

The stories haven't stopped. . .

Make Room for the Miracles

A friend recently told me about her three-year-old niece who grew up on our playground. During a beach vacation, the little girl saw another child with Down syndrome building a sandcastle. Without hesitation she trotted over, asked her name, and began to play. The other parents stared. "She's so confident. She just walked right up."

My friend told them about ESP, about the Playground of Possibilities, about a thousand small moments like this one—some on rubber surfacing, some in white sand miles away. We had hoped early, barrier-free play would create neural pathways of inclusion. Hearing it echo on a beach several hours away proved it.

The Miracle

Last December, at a mom-and-daughter Christmas tea, I chatted with a woman new to town. She studied plants across North Georgia, she said. When she asked about my work, I answered, "ESP." Her face brightened.

"I take my two-year-old to your playground almost every day. Thank you."

I smiled, always thankful for the gratitude.

"No, you don't understand." Then she lifted her pant leg show me: two prosthetic limbs.

"I was driving to do research in the mountains when I had a car accident. I woke up in the hospital with both legs gone. Your playground was the first place I could really play with my son."

I had imagined opening day: first bat hits the ball, parents cheer, kids with and without disabilities forge friendships, and a few hundred thousand neurons file a new story called *we belong together*. That would have been miracle enough. But the ripples reached further—grandparents kneeling without fear of stairs, caregivers rolling onto ramps with toddlers on their laps, parents who once hovered now playing, really playing, because the space welcomed them, too.

With God, indeed. Anything is possible.

When we exchange silos for shared spaces, "them" truly becomes "us." Lines blur. Roles bend. Neighbors discover each other. And places designed for a few become places that bless the many.

Years later, I found myself in Denver presenting with Colin, Lia, Brian, and the City of Watkinsville at a national awards ceremony. Our little city was named one of America's five All-American Cities—not for dazzling infrastructure but for shared spaces where generational miracles happen.

Silos are for storage. As a Georgia girl, I've seen them my whole life—silver spires holding grain through winter. A friend just down the road keeps barns and silos full of collectibles and treasures after selling a successful business—abundance stored with great care. Sometimes I wonder what might happen if a sliver of that abundance spilled out. How much joy it could spark, not just for others, but for him and his children. Because joy doesn't diminish when shared. It compounds.

We tend to complicate the work of belonging. But creating shared spaces is simpler than we think. Start with ABCD: What do we already have, and how can we build on it together? Look around and you'll spot the space-makers—people designing places where neighbors meet and linger. You don't need an architecture degree to be one.

Shared spaces aren't only physical. They're invitations—spoken and unspoken—that say, you belong here. There's room for you at this table, on this team, in this town.

Every day we're either shoring up silos or cultivating shared spaces. With every conversation, every greeting at a gate, every time we look someone in the eye—or look away—we're building the world we'll all have to live in.

So here's your invitation: Be a space-maker.

- **In your home:** Pull the chairs closer; leave the light on; cook one more serving.
- **In your workplace:** Ask who's not at the table and move the meeting so they can be.
- **In your neighborhood:** Turn the cul-de-sac into kickball; learn the names; host the block.
- **In your faith community:** Widen the aisle; add a ramp; make "welcome" look like action.
- **In the stands at Little League:** Cheer for every kid; tell a coach you'll help.

Start where you are. Use what you have. Build what you can. Make no small plans.

Because when we move from siloed living to shared spaces—when we plan and give and sweat toward places where everyone belongs—we don't just open a playground or stripe a ball field. We open a way of being a true community.

And in those spaces of shared belonging, we find the truest kind of joy.

That's the miracle. That's extraordinary.

CHAPTER **18**

The Top Bunk

What Happens When We Exchange Walls for Ramps?

"It's kinda fun to do the impossible."

—Walt Disney

Answer the Call

Joy was spreading. Communities were changing. From the outside, it might have looked like we had it all figured out. Far from it. The more cities we served, the more clearly I saw what we all have in common at our core: We long for community, we ache for purpose, and—if you're parenting a child with a disability—you are desperate for respite.

As ESP grew, so did the need I'd tiptoed around for years: an overnight camp of our own. We'd made do by renting space at a partner camp that served other health populations, squeezing our magic into their limited weekends, and elbowing for bunk space that disappeared the minute their calendar opened to summer. Word about ESP kept spreading, and every time we became "space makers" in a new city, the same question pressed in: If we have 10 cities, how will we serve them all? And underneath that: How will we give their families a true break?

Not everyone understands camp. Maybe you weren't the kid who sprinted from the car to be first to claim the top bunk (guilty). Maybe you're more of a retreat person—the type who works hard and retreats hard: a weekend of trail dust and hammocks, or a few lazy days by a lake. Either way, you already know the power of time away, of a pause that breathes life back into tired bones.

But what if your child will never live independently? What if you're caregiving for your child and your aging parent? One in six children has a disability. Every summer as campers check in, I see the same mix in parents' faces: giddy joy and deep trepidation. Many whisper that this is their first vacation in 12 years...or since their child was born...or ever. Travel is a privilege, yes, but not only because of money. Barriers—behavioral, physical, social—turn the simplest break into a logistical Everest.

For 20 years I've wondered: What if it didn't have to be so hard? And, as with so many of ESP's biggest leaps, curiosity took the first step.

Take the Visit

It started with a persistent man named Josh. The summer we were juggling day camp and construction on our new building, my phone lit up—again.

"I have this property," he said, voice eager. "We've been using it for a small Christian camp for adults with disabilities. We're moving to the Dominican Republic. I'd love for ESP to purchase it, only for what we owe."

"I'm sorry," I said, scanning the chaos on my desk. "I'm not interested in building an overnight camp."

He called again a few weeks later. "My board knows you're the best in the business. You could do wonderful things with this property."

I said no again.

The third time, a final plea: "Laura, my only request is that you come see it."

Relentless. I sighed. I phoned my board chair who's world-class at saying no and asked her to come so we could decline politely, in person.

The Top Bunk

One late-summer morning, #lovelikeJoseph, my board chair, and I pulled into a gravel drive. The place was quiet. Dragonflies skimmed a small lake. The air was thick with cicadas and the scent of pine and sun-warmed mud. Josh—tall, curly-haired, carrying a grin that reached both ears—walked us along dirt paths beneath heavy shade.

It wasn't perfect. Not even close. Stained mattresses. Tired bunks. A dining cabin that smelled like grease and campfire memories. A weathered pavilion. But sunlight glittered on the water, and something in my chest loosened, the way it had when I was eight and arriving at Camp Woodmont—no AC, cockroaches, a murky lake we swam in anyway. Magic doesn't require marble; it requires meaning. My favorite moment at Camp Woodmont every year? Racing to claim the top bunk. Like I'd won something.

Joseph glanced at me, the knowing look that says, *We came to say no.*

Everything in me wanted to say yes.

Two weeks later, I was on a plane to Austin, Texas, a notebook of oversized dreams balanced on my knees. Pops—Carter's dad—met me at his lake house. It was modest and bright, with wide panes of glass opening to water and trees. The kitchen table sat squarely in the sun, scarred by a thousand meals, sturdy as an old oak.

Pops has his own redemption arc. He'd built and turned around oil businesses, fought his way through alcoholism and loss, and then rebuilt his life with intention. He started a new company with shared profits for workers, met Linda at a Native American healing retreat, stitched together a blended family, and in time sold the business to create a foundation committed to places and people that make the world better.

He leaned back in a worn wooden chair, hands calloused, eyes kind and sharp. I laid it out: our families' exhaustion, the frailty of renting, the way the world is built with walls that keep our people out. I told him we wanted to build ramps instead—literal and figurative ones—so kids and parents could belong without negotiating a maze. My words felt small beside the size of the dream.

He listened. The clock ticked. Sunlight slid across the table. Then he nodded once: "I'll buy the land. You get to work."

The words hung in the air. I stared, blinking back tears.

Right there—on a quiet morning at a humble table—a dream I'd kept at arm's length took root. Pops could see it. Martha would have, too.

Envision It

Martha loved Walt Disney long before I understood why. At 19, I did not understand her Mickey shirts and avoided the paper-mâché Minnie that watched from the office. All I could see was consumerism and crowd control. Years later, #lovelikeJoseph and I took Owen to Disney—his parents' gift to us. I grumbled about heat, lines, and overpriced snacks and then climbed onto the ferry anyway with Owen on my lap, tiny fingers tucked into mine.

We rounded the bend, and Cinderella's castle rose out of Florida light. The ferry gasped all at once. I stood, lifting Owen so he could see. The smell of popcorn and cinnamon sugar wrapped Main Street; flowers overflowed their baskets; cast members waved like they'd been waiting just for us.

By plan (not mine), Owen's first ride was Space Mountain. He sobbed through the dark, and we whispered, "It gets easier from here," which may not be in Good Parenting 101 but turned out to be true.

That night, we stood behind a rope for the Dream Come True parade. Peter Pan. Ariel. Aladdin. Music swelled. The last float rounded the corner and there she was—Cinderella high on a golden pumpkin, gown shimmering like she carried the sun in her skirts. She waved. And then she looked down at me. We made eye contact. And as a tear slid down, I laughed at myself while #lovelikeJoseph grinned the "I-told-you-so" grin.

That's when I got it. Martha's love wasn't about rides or branding. It was about a place engineered for delight. A place where joy is assumed and belonging is baked into the bricks. Walt's vision began on a park bench, watching his daughters go round and round while parents waited on the sidelines. What if, he wondered, there was a place where kids and parents enjoyed it together? A place with ramps—physical, cultural, imaginative—so everyone could share delight?

ESP had become that kind of place. Pops believed we could take that spirit and build it into a home of our own.

Just Say Yes

We had gone to say no. We left saying yes.

On the other side of that yes were campers like Rosie. At her funeral, I shared one of her most joyful moments—the summer her parents finally let her try overnight camp. Rosie cried at closing ceremonies because she felt so loved she didn't want it to end. Her mother whispered and has many times since, "Every child deserves to feel what Rosie did that day at closing ceremonies."

On the other side of that yes were moms like Toni, who yes, was still in marine-like shape. She handed our team a 20-page care manifesto when she arrived, exhausted from the packing and planning it took to cross every barrier. She drove away with her stomach in her throat. What if we didn't know what her daughter, Sam, needed? That night her phone rang. She immediately answered as she slipped on her shoes, "Call 911. I'll be right there." Her heart clutched...she heard something unfamiliar. She heard laughter. Loud, unrestrained, contagious. A 19-year-old counselor had called so Mom could eavesdrop on bedtime: a cabin of girls swapping goofy jokes, Sam squealing between giggles. For the first time in her life, Sam was doing something gloriously typical—staying up late and whispering with friends, part of the magic every child should know.

On the other side of that yes were weekends like Family Camp—80 families caravaning to the coast with buddies, medical support, adaptive beach gear, and the gift of not having to be the one who thinks of everything. Parents sank into beach chairs and cried as their kids laughed in the waves and siblings built sandcastles together. We made it possible once a year by sheer force of will. But with a retreat center of our own, we could make it common.

The challenge wasn't only saying yes; it was designing a place where yes became the default. That vision pushed us to the next step: to conceive a camp that removes barriers at the blueprint.

Design the Top Bunk

With land secured, we needed more than drawings. We needed a design ethos equal to Pops' "yes," Martha's imagination, and Walt's insistence on shared delight.

Jon, the engineer on our board, phoned Dan, dean of UGA's College of Environment and Design. Could we partner with UGA and Georgia Tech to dream a truly universal camp?

Dan laughed, delighted. "Jon, the ink is still wet. We just signed an MOU with Tech to collaborate on projects that better the state. I can't think of a better one."

That fall, teams of students shuttled up and down Georgia's highways with sketchbooks and measuring tapes, listening to parents, walking our current spaces, and bending every corner toward access. I told them my favorite part of camp at eight: "claiming the top bunk." That simple memory became our lodestar. Top bunks had never been an option for many kids with physical disabilities. The students named the whole effort The Top Bunk Project—a camp where every sidewalk, building, and activity wouldn't just be compliant, they would be designed for everyone.

Their designs sang with dignity. Cabin ramps didn't live at the back; they braided the front porch into the landscape and doubled as safe pacing paths for campers with autism at night. Treehouses spiraled up in gentle arcs, so wheels and walkers and sneakers all climbed together into the canopy. The dining hall flexed: tables on gliders, seating that moved, power supply where power is actually needed, so nobody had to sit by the mop sink just to charge a device. The doors? One set—wide, beautiful, welcoming. No "accessible entrance" by the dumpsters. Parents touring the plans could picture their kids entering with everyone else because that's how the building was imagined from day one.

They wrapped the designs walkways with sensory gardens—lavender, rosemary, lamb's ear—textures and scents that grounded anxious bodies and invited delight. They imagined zipline platforms with ramps and staging areas so the moment of launch belonged to everybody, with fear and laughter braided together under clear blue sky.

That is universal design—an approach that removes barriers at the start so people can use a space to the greatest extent possible without adaptation. Not "we'll add a ramp if someone asks," but "we'll build this so the ramp is the front door." When you design that way, in buildings, programs, even relationships, togetherness happens without announcement. Everyone takes the same path. No one is steered to the margins.

Think of your world. Your home, workplace, church, or school. Where could one small ramp, literal or figurative, invite someone fully in? Move a meeting to a room without stairs. Share agendas in plain language. Put captions on the video. Ask who isn't here yet and shift so they can be. Little ramps become big welcomes.

Work the Plan

Designs in hand, we needed partners. Visionaries like Pops, encouragers like Carter, solvers like Jon. We needed community believers like Jackson EMC who wrote our first grant because they understood that wiring belonging into the grid changes everything.

We needed people like Harold. He started with $400 and built a poultry empire. Horses were his joy. He once sold a yearling for a record-breaking $3.9 million and then donated that exact amount to fund a church. A literal ramp. That was Harold: Take success, turn it into purpose. After his passing, his family formed a foundation that lifts underdogs, fuels dreams, and breaks down barriers. They'd supported ESP before, helping with the VFW building, but this time they funded the engineering to bring our camp to life. Their yes sparked another yes from a friend on the other side of the chicken industry: big dreams, bigger faith, a grit that doesn't blink at hard things. They believed in building a place where people delight in one another.

This is our biggest dream yet, our Disney-sized dream. To build it we'll need everyone: the chicken farmers and the concrete pourers, the planners and the painters, the donors and the day-volunteers. The best part? We don't know all the names yet. That's the joy of a dream like this. You start building ramps and watch who shows up on the other side.

Build the Ramp

We still have a long trail ahead. The retreat center named "Hooray" will be ESP's largest project yet: a place where adults with disabilities find meaningful employment, where families rest and play, a place for summer camp, where belonging overflows year-round. A place with a forest of ramps.

Because when you build ramps instead of walls, you move toward people. You create connection. You make room for the joy your soul keeps trying to find.

Most of us won't build a retreat center. (You could—come on over.) But each of us can build a universally designed life, one that defaults to ramps over walls.

"Uni" means one—a reminder that universal design is about one for all and all for one. In practice, everyday ramps look like:

- **At work:** Hold meetings in spaces everyone can access; share materials ahead of time; assign roles that unlock gifts—hospitality, logistics, humor—not just titles.
- **With friends:** Invite families whose calendars look complicated. Ask, "What would make this easier?" and mean it.

- **At home:** A basket of sensory tools in the den. Halloween candy at the bottom of the stairs. Teach your kids that "different" is not a warning label but an invitation.
- **In faith communities:** Turn "welcome" into a verb—larger print, quieter corners, buddy benches, ushers trained to notice who needs a hand.
- **In your own heart:** When you feel the reflex to build a wall—ignoring, avoiding, shrinking the circle—ask what ramp would lead you to love instead.

Here's the truth: You're always building something. Walls or ramps.

At 18, I stood in an office wallpapered in sticky notes with a $50,000 deficit and no clue what I was doing. I didn't see this far. But every yes—even the terrifying ones—became its own little ramp. Ramps maintaining Martha's dream. Toward new cities. Toward Java Joy. Toward Carter and Pops. Toward Harold's legacy. Toward Rosie's tears at closing ceremonies and Sam's midnight laughter, and hundreds of moments when someone felt, finally, this is for me.

Now it's your turn. Say yes. Build the ramp.

The joy exchange was never meant to bottleneck in one building or one town. It grows every time someone chooses to replace a wall with a way in. Your yes might look small, but it may be the precise ramp someone else needs to belong, to laugh, to live fully. That's how joy multiplies: one ramp, one yes, one exchanged moment at a time.

We're going to build a place where claiming the top bunk isn't a metaphor; it's a memory every camper gets to have. Where parents rest. Where siblings play. Where the path to the zipline is a spiral that welcomes the whole cabin up together. Where the front door is wide because we planned it that way. Where the dining hall hums with voices that know they are wanted.

Walt called it fun to do the impossible. I think he was telling the truth. The impossible part is real. The fun is watching a community of ordinary people decide to do it anyway—by building ramps in a world addicted to walls.

Top bunk, everyone?

CHAPTER **19**

Enjoy

What Happens When We Exchange Small Things for Big Love?

> *"Not all of us can do great things, but we can all do small things with great love."*
>
> —Mother Teresa

Accept the Invitation

We've covered so much ground together. I hope that as you've journeyed through these pages, you've felt as though you were dropped into a world just a little different from the one you live in every day. Maybe, through these stories, you've glimpsed a world where belonging is the norm, not the exception—a world where joy isn't rare or fleeting but something that can be practiced, exchanged, and multiplied.

And perhaps, somewhere along the way—as you've read about camp songs and peanut butter and jelly sandwiches, hugs and coffee carts, playgrounds and family dinners—something inside you has shifted. Maybe a few neural pathways have been rewired: old patterns softened, new habits sparked. Maybe you've found yourself looking differently at the world around you—at the people you pass in the grocery store, at the child who struggles to fit in at school, at the neighbor you've never really gotten to know. Maybe you've begun to wonder: What would it look like for me to live this way?

Because here's the truth: You can close this book, think what a nice story, and move on to the next thing in your life, forgetting the opportunity that's right in front of you.

But I hope you don't.

Over the last 20 years, across thousands of lives, I've seen something far more beautiful than most people realize. And the greatest lesson I've learned—one I owe to many of my friends at ESP—has everything to do with God.

Religion can be complicated. People are messy. Life is hard. All of that can make God feel distant, abstract, or impossible to grasp. But regardless of what you believe, there's one truth we can probably agree on—and if we really lived it out, it could change the world.

I see it when an 18-year-old counselor lifts 180 pounds of another human into the middle of a flag circle to sing a camp song—both of them smiling, delighting in one another.

I see it when a Joyrista gives a hug and offers the "question of the day," leaving someone beaming.

I see it in the soft smile of a parent who picks up their child after much-needed respite.

I see it in a CEO leaning into a nonprofit board meeting, using his skills for a purpose bigger than himself.

I see it when a mom on a playground watches her toddler play alongside a child with cerebral palsy.

I see it when a busy mother takes a moment at a stoplight to acknowledge the man holding a cardboard sign.

I see it in the young employee who spends her lunch break listening to a coworker share about raising a child with autism.

You've seen glimpses of it throughout this book, even if you couldn't quite name it.

And the question was once asked: What is the greatest commandment?

The answer was always consistent: Love God. Love your neighbor as yourself.

The greatest lesson I've learned—and the one I want to leave you with in this last chapter—is this: to enjoy others is to enjoy God, and to enjoy God is to enjoy others.

Those two commands were never meant to be separated.

The first: Love God.

The second: Love your neighbor as yourself.

It's simple enough for a child to understand yet so radical it turns the whole order of our lives upside down.

But if we're honest, we don't always know what that looks like. We debate who our "neighbor" really is. We wonder what loving God with our whole selves actually requires. We struggle to know how to begin.

The heart will grow to love what the body leans into, and the brain takes time to learn. I didn't learn the answer in a sermon or a textbook. I learned it from the very people the world often overlooks.

Let 'Em Teach

When I was 19, I took the leadership helm at ESP, a moment in time when I thought I had to be Superwoman. I even dressed up as her for Halloween at our offices. I felt the weight of my family, friends, and job, and I thought being Superwoman meant doing it all and being it all. I wasn't even sure what my "superpowers" were. I believed leadership meant holding everything together, never letting anyone down, and proving that I was capable of every single role.

But the greatest power I was learning to see was right under my nose.

While culture cheers for strength, independence, and achievement, I've discovered that the ones culture often calls weak or unaccomplished are the very people who have taught me the most important powers.

At 18, I met a camper with a contagious smile. He loved superheroes, sports, fashion, and—of course—girls. Our young male counselors would bring him to camp early, wheel his thin body into our two-stall bathroom, comb his hair into a stylish 'do, dress him in camp clothes (often a Superman shirt), and then whip him out of the bathroom, transformed—like a superhero.

Superman hosted a "kissing booth" during Fair Day. He charged for each kiss on the cheek to raise money for summer camp. His unit won the fundraising competition that year—no surprise there.

When I first stepped into leadership at ESP, still a college student myself, I wanted to play, to engage, to soak up the joy that had first drawn me in. But as a leader, I found myself behind a desk, buried in paperwork and phone calls, longing for that same connection.

And every day, Superman found a way to remind me why I was there.

Each hot Georgia afternoon, around 12:20, after hours of adrenaline-filled camp activity, I'd be in that tiny office when I heard his slow, distinct, cerebral-palsy-toned voice call out. . .

"Laaaaaaauuuuuura!"

Within days, he'd trained me.

It was time to set everything down.

I'd sit with him, tearing up pieces of the peanut butter and jelly sandwich his buddy made, feeding him bite by bite. I'd often forget to eat my own lunch because, in those moments, a deeper hunger was satisfied.

Every day, he ended our time together with the same words:

"Laaaaurrra. I love you."

Superman knew what I needed. Not a mental-health break. Not scrolling my phone. Not a protein shake or a quick walk.

I needed a human moment—a reminder that I was loved.

The late Bell Hooks once wrote in *All About Love*:

> "Taught to believe that the mind, not the heart, is the seat of learning, many of us believe that to speak of love with any emotional intensity means we will be perceived as weak and irrational."[1]

Her book remained largely unnoticed until her death, when—21 years after it was published—it became a *New York Times* bestseller. The timing made sense. We live in a culture desperate for her message:

> "It is especially hard to speak of love when doing so calls attention to the fact that lovelessness is more common than love, and that many of us are not sure what we mean when we talk of love or how to express it."[2]

Researcher Brené Brown puts it this way: "Love is not attention. Attention is easy. Love is sacred. Attention can be given without care. Love requires presence, consistency, and emotional safety. Attention is a performance. Love is a practice."[3]

We live in a world obsessed with attention—who noticed me, who complimented me, who "liked" my post. But attention isn't love.

Love isn't loud. It's quiet, steady, and unglamorous. It demands presence. It's awkward sometimes. It's practiced—until it becomes who we are.

Jesus calls it the greatest commandment.

Culture often sees it as a weakness.

Brené reminds us it's not attention—it's a practice.

So who's practicing it? And where do we see it?

Make the Hole

A few years later, Superman graduated high school. He could no longer ride the school bus to camp, so our staff drove to his rural county every morning to pick him up—lifting his fragile body, loading his wheelchair into the truck bed, making it back just in time for our 8 a.m. staff meeting. In the afternoons, they'd drive him home, windows rolled down in the Georgia heat.

We would do whatever it took to get him to camp.

And when there was no way, we made a hole.

Because when you love—and when you know you're loved—you start tearing through roofs to lower people in, just to get them what they need.

Then one day, Superman was gone.

His family moved again. The number we had no longer worked. After countless calls, there was silence.

No one knew where he was.

For three years, I searched for him. Seasons came and went without a sign of my hero. We served hundreds of campers, but the "lost sheep" was still lost. I often thought about his mom, who had him as a teenager. What if she'd had support? Another family walking the same path? Resources that could have kept them stable? A place where she felt loved?

Love requires action.

As social psychologist Erich Fromm said, "Love is an active power in a man. Love is, as love does."[4]

And as pastor Andy Stanley often asks, "What does love require of me?"

Superman's absence led us to create ESP's Family Support Program—our hole in the roof. Today, every new family receives a welcome call, a personal meeting, invitations to family dinners, scholarships, counseling, trips, and, most importantly, community.

Let Love Lead

One day, years later, I toured a nonprofit serving seniors. While visiting their adult day program, I shook hands and exchanged smiles with elderly participants.

And then—out of the corner of my eye—I saw a familiar face, albeit a bearded one.

My legs started running before my brain caught up. Tears streamed down my face.

And then I heard it—the voice I'd been aching to hear for years:

"Laaaaaaaaaura. . . ..ESP, ESP, ESP. I loooooove you!"

There was my Superman—healthy, cared for, and still loving big.

We spent the afternoon reminiscing, planning his return to ESP. The staff around us—now part of his story—listened, smiling at tales of his legendary kissing booth.

As I listened, I learned he had to leave his home so that his care could be a priority. And yet, I was amazed by the stories his friends shared—tales of joy sparked by his love for them, far beyond our walls. Even in the years we couldn't find him, Superman, true to form, was out changing lives everywhere he went.

That summer, Superman came home.

Back to camp.

Back to the place where his superpower—love—could shine.

In Atlas of the Heart, Brené Brown writes, "Love and belonging are irreducible needs for all people. In the absence of these experiences, there is always suffering. We need more real love—gritty, dangerous, wild-eyed, justice-seeking love."[5]

Love is a superpower. But every Superman has kryptonite.

Ours is often ourselves—our self-focus, our desire for comfort, our fear of rejection, our obsession with control, achievement, and appearances.

The greatest enemy to your joy. . .is you.

And yet, all around you is opportunity—

the house down the street,

the man at the light,

the bagger at the checkout,

the mom at PTO,

the employee from a different generation,

the new family at school,

the kid on your team who feels left out,

the family whose child has just received the autism diagnosis.

I hope you'll lean in. This is your neighborhood. These are your neighbors.

And the joy exchange is waiting for you.

Love is like a dandelion seed—small, ordinary, easy to miss. But when the wind carries it, it finds new soil, takes root, and grows in the most unexpected places. That's how joy spreads. That's how communities change. That's how the world becomes new.

One of my favorite quotes is from Mother Teresa: "Not all of us can do great things, but we can all do small things with great love."[6]

My hope is that you'll choose a love that may be small but bold enough to build ramps and tear open roofs—a love willing to move from awkward to aha, from invisible to invaluable, from them to us. Because the small, daily seeds of love are what grow into the big things.

When you live this way, you'll discover your most significant power isn't in what you achieve or control. It's in delighting in the person right in front of you. It's in discovering God's love for you as you pour it out on someone else above yourself. It was, after all, the first exchange His Son gave in human form.

Then, and only then, do we find the one word it all boils down to—the thing we are all searching for—a life we desire, and yet we look in all the wrong places. It's the word our Joyristas say as they hand you your coffee, your hug, as both a blessing and an invitation. It's a word I leave with you as you step into your own joy exchange. . .

Enjoy.

Any part of your life exchanged for joy is a part of your life enjoyed.

Epilogue

Welcome to Holland

To those who have experienced something different in life than what you expected...this is for you.

When a new family joins the ESP family, we give them a poem.

The poem was written by Emily Pearl Kingsley and is known around the world. In it, she compares having a baby to planning a dream trip to Italy. You spend months preparing—buying travel books (or today, consulting ChatGPT), mapping out every detail of your journey. You picture yourself at the Colosseum, gliding through Venice on gondolas, savoring the food, even learning a bit of Italian.

But after all that anticipation, you board the plane, land, and hear the pilot say, "Welcome to Holland."

Kingsley's poem beautifully captures the heartbreak of unmet expectations when you have a child with a disability. You've dreamed your whole life of Italy, and now you're in an entirely different place. Maybe your own journey has taken an unexpected turn.

Yet as you begin to explore the land you never planned to visit, something happens. You see the windmills. You discover Rembrandts. You notice the tulips.

At every new family meeting, we sit with parents who find themselves on that unexpected flight. We hand them tulips as we share a truth we've come to know—yes, Holland is different. But in so many ways, it can be more breathtaking than they ever imagined.

Life is often navigated in black and white. Even the pages of this book are black and white. But as you close it and look at the cover in color, I hope you'll remember one thing through one sweet face—the face of Suzanne on the back cover.

Suzanne is a bright-eyed, athletic, giggly friend who always has her nails painted and a summer tan. She lives in athleisure, gives the best hugs, and creates art that bursts with color. She also has

Down syndrome. Suzanne is one of our Joyristas and loves to paint flowers—daisies, sunflowers, tulips.

Her life has been marked by open-heart surgeries, the loss of her mom to cancer, and challenges most of us will never know. And yet she graces the world with her spark—cup by cup, brushstroke by brushstroke. Just months after her mom passed away, she painted me a picture of a dandelion. Long before this book was even an idea, she placed it in my hands. Today, it sits behind my desk, reminding me—and now you, as the cover of this book—to consider the wildflowers:

> "Consider the wildflowers. They don't labor or spin. Yet I tell you, not even Solomon in all his splendor was dressed like one of these."

This upside-down truth—Israel's third monarch, the famous King Solomon, the picture of wealth and power, outshone by wildflowers—still stuns me. What were they wearing? Perhaps the same thing I've seen in Suzanne's art and in the stories of this book.

Pure radiance.

Here is what joy does—if we choose it, even in the unexpected, it clothes us. Not in fabric, but in light. A light that cannot be held, only shared. A light that, when we choose to delight in one another, spills onto those around us.

Joy is not found in the life we planned, but in the life we are given with those around us.

Joy is leaning into the awkward and rewiring our rhythms. Joy is discovering our best selves in serving—and finding the love of a neighbor in return.

Joy is the unexpected friendship and the camaraderie of ramp building together.

Joy is seeing the dandelions—and the people who surprise us by becoming family.

It is when we choose to delight in one another—exchanging "them" for "us"—we find that we are dressed in something far greater than anything money can buy or culture can offer. We are clothed in pure radiance, more valuable than all the money, fame, or wisdom in the world can buy.

We are clothed in joy.

The Invitation

Joy multiplies when it's shared.
You've just read stories of miracles, courage, and contagious love. The same kind of joy is still unfolding every day through the work of **Extra Special People (ESP)**—a place where barriers fall and belonging rises.

The *Joy Exchange Fund* exists so that no dreamer is left waiting, no family is left alone, and no community misses the chance to experience radical joy.
If you've ever wondered how to make the world a little lighter—this is your invitation.

Join the Joy Exchange.
Give. Serve. Share.
Because joy is only complete when it's given away.

Donate at www.espyouandme.org/joyexchangefund

Notes

Section Three
1. Fromm, E. (1956). *The Art of Loving*, 25. New York: Harper & Row.

Chapter 1
1. Clear, J. (2018). *Atomic Habits*, 27. New York: Avery.

Chapter 2
1. Brown, B. (2022). *Atlas of the Heart: Mapping Meaningful Connection and the Language of Human Experience*, 95. New York: Crown Publishing.
Schore, A.N. (1994). *Affect Regulation and the Origin of the Self: The Neurobiology of Emotional Development*. Hillsdale, NJ: Lawrence Erlbaum Associates.
2. Wilder, J. (2013). *Joy Starts Here: The Transformation Zone*. East Peoria, IL: Shepherd's House.
3. Lewis, C.S. (1950). *The Lion, the Witch and the Wardrobe*. London: Geoffrey Bles.
4. Plakias, A. (2023). *Awkwardness: And Other Essays*. New York: Oxford University Press.
5. Troilus and Cressida, Act I, Scene iii.

Chapter 3
1. Prov. 14:4 (English Standard Version).

Chapter 4
1. Einstein to Carl Seelig, March 11, 1952; quoted in Walter Isaacson, *Einstein: His Life and Universe*, 548.

Chapter 6
1. Goetz, Keltner, and Simon-Thomas, *The Oxford Book of Compassion*. 2010, p. 351.
2. Singer, T. and Klimecki, O.M. (2017). Empathy and compassion. In: *The Oxford Handbook of Compassion* (ed. E.M. Seppälä, E. Simon-Thomas, S.L. Brown, et al.). (Oxford: Oxford University Press.
3. Darwin.
4. Warneken and Tomasello 2006, 1301.

Chapter 8
1. Marshall Terrill, "The Science of Hope: More Than Wishful Thinking," *ASU News*, June 15, 2021.

Chapter 9
1. Ruskin, J. (1856). *Modern Painters*, vol. 3, 27. London: Smith, Elder & Co.

Chapter 11
1. Brown, B. and Greatly, D. (2012). *How the Courage to Be Vulnerable Transforms the Way We Live, Love, Parent, and Lead.* New York: Gotham Books.
2. Roosevelt, E. (1960). *You Learn by Living: Eleven Keys for a More Fulfilling Life.* New York: Harper & Brothers.

Chapter 13
1. Boyle, G. (2010). *Tattoos on the Heart: The Power of Boundless Compassion.* New York: Free Press.

Chapter 14
1. Clear, J. (2018). *Atomic Habits: An Easy & Proven Way to Build Good Habits & Break Bad Ones*, 38. New York: Avery.

Chapter 15
1. Mooney, A. (1995). Four hugs a day using therapeutic touch. *British Journal of Theatre Nursing* 5 (7): 25–27.

Chapter 16
1. Schore, A. N. (2000). Attachment and the regulation of the right brain. *Attachment and Human Development*, 2(1), 23–47.
2. Wilder, J. and Friesen, K. (2013). *Joy Starts Here: The Transformation Zone*. Pasadena, CA: Shepherd's House.

Chapter 19
1. Bell Hooks. (2000). *All About Love: New Visions*. New York: HarperCollins.
2. Ibid.
3. Brown, B. (2021). *Atlas of the Heart: Mapping Meaningful Connection and the Language of Human Experience*. New York: Random House.
4. Fromm, E. (1956). *The Art of Loving*. New York: Harper & Row.
5. Brown, B. (2021). *Atlas of the Heart: Mapping Meaningful Connection and the Language of Human Experience*. New York: Random House.
6. Teresa, M. (1997). *A Simple Path* (ed. L. Vardey). New York: Ballantine Books.

Acknowledgments

A mentor once told me, "Write this down so this magic can go further than you can walk."

God planted the seed of this book in my heart—not only to fund the work we do but to spark opportunities for love in every community: home, neighborhood, office, and church.

Many people watered that seed: early in life, my parents, and siblings. For all of my career, my husband and now children who are so deeply invested. My co-authors, those I thought I was serving who ended up serving me. My mentors and team members over the years who dreamed big and rolled up their sleeves beside me.

In the final stretch, I'm especially grateful for the partners who helped this book come to bloom: Steve, Heather, Morgan, Leah, Brent, Wiley, and the generous donors who believed in me, in this story, so it could be shared with anyone willing to join it.

May the one seed become many—gifting the opportunity for joy wherever it lands.

About the Author

Laura Hope Whitaker, M.Ed., is the CEO of Extra Special People, Inc. (ESP), a nonprofit transforming communities through belonging for individuals with disabilities and their families. Laura began as a volunteer and counselor in college and, at just 19 years old, stepped into leadership following the founder's passing. Under her direction, ESP has grown into a nationally recognized organization with innovative programs like Java Joy and SeeAbility.

A passionate voice and speaker, Laura has delivered a TEDx talk, *The Dandelion Shift*, and has been recognized as one of Georgia Most Admired CEOs by the *Atlanta Business Chronicle* and Georgia Trend's *40 Under 40* and *UGA's 40 under 40* and *Alumna of Distinction Top 100*. She has also served on the governor-appointed GBHDD Board and currently serves as a leader at Athens Church and on the board of directors for the Oconee State Bank.

Laura holds bachelor's and master's degrees in special education from the University of Georgia. Beyond her professional accomplishments, her favorite role is wife to Joseph and mom to Owen, Finley, and Tate. Laura wakes every day to lean in with big love, shifting hope-filled perspectives that build joy-filled communities.

Index

A

ability
  appearing in unexpected forms, 88
  exchange of inability for, 87, 95
  naming of, 92, 150
  seeing, 94–95
administrative support, 37
"age of bad generalization" (Brooks concept), 85
"Ain't No Mountain High Enough" (song), 113
All About Love (hooks), 192
All-American Cities award, 175
Allen wrenches, 121
American Idol, 78
America's Got Talent, 78
amygdala, 98
Angelou, Maya, 121
anger, 53
anticipation, 123
Arizona State University, 67–68
The Art of Loving (Fromm), 119
The Art of "Us," 120
asset-based community development (ABCD), 171, 176
attention vs. love distinction, 193
awkwardness
  aha transformation, 146, 152
  concerns about, 89

  cure for, 24
  as emotional radar, 15
  hesitation of, 27
  insight from, 78
  invitation of socially awkward encounters, 25
  leaning into, 8, 17, 164
  as social barrier, 14
  as social cue, 23
  softening of, 82

B

beauty, 126, 130
becoming through doing, 112
bees, 64
belonging, 122, 138, 149, 159–160, 195
  and connection, 5
  and joy, 177, 182–183
  kids needing, 106
  and love, 195
  as norm, 189
  and perfection, 174
  rising, 199
  shared spaces, 176–177
  as strongest driver of engagement, 128
bias, 88
Big Hearts, 78–80, 82–85, 89, 156

The Big Jump, 99, 101
big love, 104
Biscoff cookie moment, 146–147
Bitty & Beau's Coffee, 164
blends, 133–142
blind date, 41–48
board of directors, 38
"body keeps the score"
    metaphor, 107
bonds of summer camp, 33
Bouncing Beans
    (coffee stand), 134
Boyle, G., 129
brags
  as discipline of sight, 95
  tradition, 91
Braves midseason-trades
    metaphor, 171–173
breaking social stiffness, 7
Bridgestone, 3
brookies (brownie-cookie
    hybrids), 172
Brooks, David, 27, 85, 140
The Brothers Trust (Tom
    Holland's
    foundation), 6, 162
Brothers Trust Ball, 163
Brown, Brené, 9, 21, 104,
    138, 193, 195
Bryce, Crystal, 67
bursts, 11–17, 27
butterfly metaphor, 81, 174
"buy the glasses" story,
    19–20

C
Cathy, Dan, 150–151
Channel 2 (news), 147
Chick-fil-A True Inspiration
    Award, 150
childhood memory, 11
Chinmoy, Sri, 41
chromosomal deletion (rare), 47
Clear, James, 15, 139
college counselors, 50
comfort, pairing new
    experience with, 139
communication
  augmentative device, 81
  nonverbal, 79
community
  building, 176–177
  exposure, 89
  gathering, 100–102
  investment, 116
  longing for purpose, 179
  outburst, 38
  steps toward, 62
companionship, desire for, 41
compassion
  as action, 54
  brain malleability through, 149
  children learning, 15
  diagram, 55
  human touch and, 149
connection
  and ant colonies, 171
  over compliance, 129
  created with intention, 142
  exchanging culture
    for, 143–153
  positive, 168
constants, repetition yields, 151
construction learning
    vocabulary, 111
contagiousness, 155

cooperation and interdependence, 54
"corporate partner days," 133
courage
　borrow, 103, 105
　as contagious momentum, 102
　continuum, 106
　vs. cowardice, 97
　expansion, 99
　personal and collective, 105
　slow-motion courage of parenting, 102
　stories, 102
COVID-19 pandemic, 155, 158, 159, 172
cowardice vs. courage, 97
cultural misunderstanding of service, 29
culture vs. genuine perception, 9
curiosity, 35, 180

D
daffodils, 119
dandelions, 63, 119
　as ecosystem contributors, 120
　magic of, 3
　medicinal uses, 3
　metaphor, 133, 195
　as nutrient providers, 64
　painting, 198
Darwin, Charles, 54
David, Susan, 57
decisive action, 17
delight vs. disgust, 126
Dempsey, Gaines, 159
Descent of Man (Darwin), 54
DiCaprio, Leonardo, 6
Dion, Celine, 6

disability
　adults with, 52, 142, 144, 148
　employment barriers for people with, 156
　feeling safe to disclose, 141
　perceptions, 89
　representation of, 77
　revealing divine qualities, 45
　statistics, 134
　stories, 138
discomfort, 60–62
　binds us together, 58
　vs. danger differentiation, 16
Disney, 60, 182
Disney Channel, 57
Disney, Walt, 179, 182
Dooley, Barbara, 71
Dooley, Vince, 71, 100
Dowdle, Chuck, 71
dreaming for others, 167
dream vs. reality, 65

E
Eckhart, Meister, 107
Einstein, Albert, 13, 40
emotional contagion, 157, 160, 164
emotional equity, 127
empathy, 53–56
endurance and confidence building, 58
"epidemic of loneliness," 62
Erasmus, Desiderius, 167
ESP. *See* Extra Special People (ESP)
Excel spreadsheet waitlist, 50

experience
  family trip, 11
  opportunity vs., 29
  positive, 168
  shaping perception, 4
extra seat metaphor, 19
Extra Special People (ESP), 8, 21–25, 48, 50, 59, 69, 77, 84, 89, 109, 149, 156, 159, 172, 179, 186, 190, 191, 197, 199
  anthem, 28
  Club, 27
  Family Support Program, 194
  origin story, 34

F
falling vs. floating metaphor, 98–99
family as expanded community, 19
Family Support Program (ESP), 194
fear, 97–100, 102–106, 185
filling the cup metaphor, 76
flip turn
  instruction, 57
  metaphor, new momentum, 61
friendship, 15, 16, 50–51, 57–58, 62, 156
  -based collaboration, 37–38
  -led hospitality, 89
  through connection, 32
Fromm, Erich, 119, 194

G
Georgia foundations, 75
Georgia Theatre, 71, 89, 90

The Giving Tree (book), 93
global mobile-security conference, 144
goodness, naming, 92
good touch, relearning, 149
grief, 34
Groban, Josh, 47
Guidara, Will, 127
guilt, carried into adulthood, 125
"gut-wrenching grocery" phase, 59

H
habit formation through bursts, 13
Hallmark, 84
handprints, in concrete, 116–118
harmony, 119
help, asking for, 36
"Here Comes the Sun" theme, 159
Hill, Patrick, 140
Holland, Don, 6
Holland, Nikki, 6, 162
Holland, Paddy, 6
Holland, Sam, 6
Holland, Tom, 162
holy ground metaphor, 88
hooks, bell, 192
hope, 65–76, 158
  as discipline, 67
  fulfillment of, 70
  metaphors, 70, 71
  as motion, 76
  vs. optimism, 68
  "putting hope to work," 68
  requires responsibility and action, 68

social nature of, 75
as spark and fuel, 68
strategy, 76
hospitality, 121, 123, 125–131, 133
Hot Corner (coffee shop), 45–46
hubris
origin from Greek mythology, 43
in religious interpretation, 45
as societal danger, 43
Hug Counter, 161
hugs, 136–138, 143–153, 158, 190
human touch and compassion, 149
humility
vs. hubris, 43
as lifelong companion, 48
spectrum, 43

I

identity shifts, built on small votes, 139
ignorance vs. unwillingness, 72
IKEA, 121
inadequacy
awkward, 35
exposing, 36
in professional settings, 38
inclusion, neural pathways of, 168, 174
inclusive celebration, 7
inclusive classrooms vs. adult environments, 139
inclusive play research, 168
individualism vs. joy, 120

infants, compassion observed at 18 months, 55
insecurity
affirmation during, 32
in young adulthood, 21
Instagram, 36
intellectual disability, 44
interconnectedness of nature, 120
interdependence, 54
intuition
as gift, 17
leadership, 15–16
as moral signal, 14
neuroscience and, 13
vs. rational mind, 13
intuitive burst, 16
invisible burdens, 138
invisible to invaluable metaphor, 64, 76, 95, 115, 152
invitation vs. wanting, 121
isolation, 40
health risks of, 62
Ivy League, 143

J

Java Joy, 138–142
Atlanta, 160
championing, 150
Coffee. Hug. Enjoy, 151, 153
first encounter, 144
hugs, 152
need for vehicles, 156
as social enterprise, 161
story, 134
swag, 146
"Jesus Loves Me" (song), 44
Johnson, Matthew Kuan, 8

joy
  through action, 25, 199
  in awkward, 198
  becomes culture, 164
  and belonging, 177, 182–183
  capacity, 22, 163
  at closing ceremonies, 183
  clothed in, 198
  as clothing us in light, 198
  as contagious, 163, 164
  definition of, 9
  exchange, 9, 17, 196
  on far side of hesitation, 131
  and free coffee, 147
  Friday joy, 157
  as global language, 163
  vs. happiness, 9, 143, 151
  importance of, 24
  increasing productivity, 134
  vs. individualism, 120
  as life-changing insight, 8
  as "light," 9
  math of, 165
  missed, 23
  moving through teams, 116
  multiplies (when shared), 187, 199
  as persuasive, 157
  pilot-light joy metaphor, 164
  portable, 161
  as practice, 189
  as radiant phenomenon, 144, 152
  refusing to stay in one place, 150
  in serving, 198
  as social connector, 7
  sparking, 94
  spreading, 155, 179, 195
  transformative power of, 167
  traveling across generations, 158
Joy Exchange Fund, 199
joyful hospitality, 127, 130
JP Morgan Chase, 148
Jung, Carl, 87

K
Keltner, Dacher, 149
Kingsley, Emily Pearl, 197
kinship begins with delight, 129
kintsugi (Japanese golden joinery), 109

L
labels, flattening curiosity, 16
Lama, Dalai, 146, 155
laughter
  as bonding, 57–58
  and fear, 185
leadership, 15–16, 29, 30, 48, 103–105, 108, 109, 113, 172, 191
Lee, Bruce, 77
Lewis, C.S., 9, 22
life, acquiring stage of, 143
lifesaver game, 57
"light low, eyes level" metaphor, 86
Lindsay, Duke and Tammy, 158
LinkedIn, 36
listening, 86
Little Debbies, 60
lost sheep metaphor, 194

loudness and quiet strength, contrast between, 48
love
 active power of, 194
 vs. attention, 193
 and belonging, 195
 as practice, 193
 requiring action, 194
 requiring presence, 193
 as superpower, 195
love God/love neighbor, 190, 198
#lovelikeJoseph, 48, 80, 98, 107, 181
Love on the Spectrum (TV show), 164
Lucky Charms, 59

M

marriage restoration, 45
Mauss, Marcel, 116
McDonald's, 12
Memory, Jelani, 133
mental playlist metaphor, 73
mentorship, 36–38
Mercedes-Benz Stadium, 160
messiness of cleansing metaphor, 108
Microsoft Word, 78
Middle-Younger group, 28
miracle, 167–177
Miracle League
 field, 170
 in Georgia, 168
momentum building, 75
Montessori, Maria, 117

movement begins with small seeds, 133
multimillion-dollar campaign, launch of, 169
muscular dystrophy, 82
"My Heart Will Go On" (song), 6

N

neighbors, 190–191, 195
Netflix, 84
neural pathways
 of inclusion, 168, 174
 new, 139
 rewiring, 13
neuroscience and intuition, 13
Newton, Isaac, 97
"Night That Could Change It All," 93
noise-canceling headphones, 129
Number Seven (construction superintendent), 113–114, 125

O

open seat metaphor, 25
opportunities, missed, 12, 17
optimism vs. hope, 68
outside force (Newton metaphor), 97
overwhelm, managing, 37
Oxford Handbook of Compassion, 54

P

Parsi, John, 67
perfect imperfection, 47

Perry, Bruce, 20
perseverance, 74
pie metaphor, 46
pink hard hat, as
    metaphor, 107–118
Plakias, Alexandra, 23
playground
    design (ordinary vs.
        extraordinary), 169
    elements, 173
    universally designed, 168
"Playground of Possibilities,"
    169, 172–174
Pollack, David, 83
positive experiences, 168
posture and perspective, 86
power for perspective, 85
precision vs. unpredictability, 82
"pretzel hold," 30
problem-solving, 39, 40
production effect
    (psychology), 92
professionalism, 145
proximity, 127, 138, 164
purpose
    exchanging problem
        for, 133–142
    as impact on others, 140
    vs. profession, 135

Q
QuickBooks, 87

R
radiance, 198
radiant reciprocity, 116, 118
rational thinking, 16

recession impact, 52
reciprocity, 115, 116, 118
recreation programs, lack of
    accessibility in, 122
Redmoon, Ambrose
    Hollingworth, 97
relationship, 62
    vs. retreat, 61
respite, parents needing, 53, 179
revolution, simple human
    exchange as, 153
ribbon-cutting ceremony, 124
Richt, Mark, 83
Roosevelt, Eleanor, 33, 105
Roosevelt, Theodore, 35, 105
RoundUp, 3
Ruskin, John, 85

S
Sam's Club, 46
scarcity mindset, 74, 100
school bus incident, 20
Schore, Allan, 22, 163
second mountain (Brooks), 140
seed/trunk metaphor, 124
seeing the unseen, 64
seeing vs. being seen, 80
Seinfeld, Jerry, 126
self-doubt and opportunity, 29
self-focus, 195
self-sufficiency, 38
separation, as source of
    anxiety, 119
Serendipity (film), 43
service, as destiny
    discovery, 29–30
Shakespeare, William, 19, 24

shared delight, as social wiring, 22
shared spaces
  as belonging, 176
  as invitation, 176
  vs. silos, 167–177
sharing people's stories vs. data, 38
ship metaphor, 104
sign language, 16
silos
  breaking, 170–171
  vs. shared spaces, 167–177
  as storage, 176
"Skinnamarinky-dinky-dink" (song), 27
Smart, Kirby, 83
Smith, Nick, 84
social bonds, evolution of, 54
social capital, 116
social connection and rhythm, 58
social fear, 103
social isolation, health risks of, 62
social urge, 54
sound as language, 79
"space makers," in new cities, 179
Special Olympics, 57–59
speech device, 31
spring recital, 103
Stanford Medicine's Center for Compassion and Altruism Research and Education, 54
Stanley, Andy, 194
"sticky-note donor," 78
sticky notes, 33–40, 72
suffering, reducing, 54
synchronized peer bonding, 51

T

"taking a knee as respect" phrase, 82–83
talent show (Goon vs. Hulk match), 51
teacher-in-training program, 15
technology, reducing social practice, 23
Teresa, Mother, 49, 189, 196
testudo formation (Roman battle strategy), 74
theater event impact, 80
"them" for "us," exchange of, 198
time-zone reset moment, 144
Titanic (film), 6
The Top Bunk Project, 184
tortoise formation. *See* testudo formation
touch, 149, 151, 152
trauma, 149
transformative experiences, for people with disabilities, 8
transgenerational transmission, 140
Transmetropolitan (pizza pub), 43
trauma, 149
traveling coffee cart idea, 134
tree of life (hope fulfilled metaphor), 70
True Inspiration Award, 150

turtle emoji, 74
Tutu, Desmond, 65, 143, 152

U

unemployment, 144
United Way, 38
universal design, 185, 186
University of Georgia (UGA), 21, 41, 44, 58, 82
unpredictability vs. precision, 82
unreasonable hospitality, 127
upside-down truth (Solomon vs. wildflowers), 198
U.S. Army War College, 68
U.S. Surgeon General, 62
"us vs. them," humans dividing, 119
utility-bill "round up" fund, 40

V

vaccination events, 159
venture capital, 143
VFW club, 88
visibility problem (roof vs. stage), 89
vision, 169, 170
visionary/encourager/solver roles, 185
volunteers, 66
vulnerability, 31, 39, 109

W

Wall Street, 143
walls vs. ramps metaphor, 187
Watkinsville, Georgia, 21
Webber, Jeremy, 68
weeds (as social metaphor), 3
weed vs. flower narrative, 63–64
weightlessness in water, 57
welcome calls, 194
welcome culture, 130
"Welcome to Holland" (poem by Kingsley), 197
"We'll see ya—at Bulldog Kia!" (commercial tagline), 156
"what breaks your heart fixes your eyes," 108
Whip and Nae Nae (dance), 73
White Apron Ceremony, 149–150
wholeness, myth of, 118
Wilder, Jim, 22, 163
wildflowers as metaphor, 198
Wilson, Lainey, 84
Winslet, Kate, 6
workplace culture ratings, highest in 10 years, 137
work, purpose in, 114
Wyllie, Martha, 124

Y

You Are My Sunshine (song), 84
"You Raise Me Up" (song), 47